DIVINE PALACES OF SOUTH INDIA

VOLUME 2
The Dancing Temples of Karnataka

Irene Black was born and educated in England and has lived and travelled extensively around the world. Formerly a psychologist and teacher, she has an MA in Asian arts and as well as this two-volume guide to Hindu temples in southern India, she has written three novels and a biography.

Also by Irene Black

DIVINE PALACES OF SOUTH INDIA
VOLUME 1
A Guide to understanding the Hindu Temple

Biography

If only I could have News from you: *Two refugees of the Nazi era share their extraordinary lives through letters and documents*

Three novels that explore cross-cultural relationships:

The Moon's Complexion

Darshan: A journey

Noontide Owls

DIVINE PALACES OF SOUTH INDIA

Irene Black

VOLUME 2
The Dancing Temples of Karnataka

GOLDENFORD

Goldenford Publishers Ltd
Guildford
www.goldenford.co.uk

First published in Great Britain in 2019 by
Goldenford Publishers Limited
The Old Post Office
130 Epsom Road Guildford
Surrey GU1 2PX
Tel: 01483 563307
Fax: 01483 604222
www.goldenford.co.uk

Cover design by the author

ISBN 978-1-911317-05-0

CONTENTS

AUTHOR'S NOTE

In 2005 I graduated with distinction from De Montfort University in Leicester, UK, with a Masters degree by independent study in South Asian arts. The following chapters, which make up Volume 2 of a two-part series on Indian Temple architecture, are based upon research carried out for my dissertation on Hoysala Temples. Volume 1 consists of five essays that give an introduction to the art and architecture of South Indian temples.

ACKNOWLEDGEMENTS

Without my son Antony's initiative this work would not exist, since it was he who placed before me the details of Dr Crispin Branfoot's Oxford University Summer School course on Indian temple architecture. It was this inspirational course that convinced me to continue my studies in this area and I will be forever grateful to Antony for suggesting it and to Crispin for subsequently offering to take me on as a somewhat mature MA student at De Montfort University.

Thanks are also due to so many for their help and advice: Dr N S Rangaraju of Mysore University and the late Dr Gerard Foekema for their advice on Hoysala temples; IISc student Sunitha for clambering cheerfully with me through python-infested ruins; our driver, Raju, who drove us safely across the length and breadth of rural Karnataka, often to the detriment of his car's health, but who took it all uncomplainingly in his stride. I would particularly like to express my gratitude to Prof M S Shaila for her assistance and friendship during my sojourns at the Indian Institute of Science in Bangalore and her companionship on our travels.

Thank you, Jennifer Margrave, Jacquelynn Luben and Frances Craddock at Goldenford for supporting and expediting this undertaking.

Lastly, thank you to my daughter, Joanna, for her photographic input and simply for being there for me.

I dedicate this volume and its companion to my late husband Donald, who shared and fostered my love of India, and who trudged endlessly around Karnataka with me in search of temples, sharing my enthusiasm from start to finish and providing me with invaluable words of wisdom.

The Dancing Temples
of Karnataka

Introduction

The area around Mysore in southern Karnataka was the heartland of the Hoysala dynasty during the 12th and 13th centuries CE. The name has become synonymous with a large number of temples built in these territories during this time. The Hoysala "style" has become associated with star-shaped temples with prolific, finely detailed carving on exterior walls, often standing on a platform. This book, based on my MA thesis, explores the genesis of these temples and aims to establish whether they constitute a distinct style or whether they are an inevitable evolution from temples previously established in Karnataka that started with the Early Chalukyas in the sixth century. The immediate predecessors of the Hoysalas were the Later Chalukyas, and for the much of the 12th century they were still in power in parts of northern Karnataka, centred in Kalyani (Kalyana). Prior to overthrowing them in 1192 the Hoysalas were their feudatories. Therefore the influence of Later Chalukya architecture on Hoysala temples is particularly interesting. Some scholars do not, in fact, distinguish between the two.In the following chapters I have identified features that are unique to Hoysala temples and those from earlier periods that the Hoysala architects popularised and developed to such an extent that they have become integral to their temples. A further aim of my studies was to establish whether these features developed independently or whether there is a connection between them. My analysis is centred on twelve temples in the Hoysala heartland that span much of the Hoysala era, having been built between 1113 CE and 1268 CE. These beautiful temples would be of as much interest to tourists as to art historians, and a wonderful introduction to the Hoysala heartlands for anyone visiting Bangalore or Mysore.

Fig 1: Largest cities and selected historical sites in the Deccan and South India

Chapter 1: The Hoysalas: who were they?

Fig 2. Chennakesava Temple, Belur: 1117 CE the Hoysala crest,
Sala fighting the tiger

To understand the Hoysalas we must throw some light on their origins and the boundaries within which most of their temples are found. Only then can we visualise them in their historical and geographical context. Equally important to our understanding is a grasp of the other dynasties in power in the area during the mediaeval period between the 6th and 14th centuries. The Hoysalas were a relatively minor dynasty in

South Karnataka, but are renowned for their contribution to art and architecture, notably in the many amazing temples that they constructed between the beginning of the 12th and the first two-thirds of the 13th centuries. Fig 3 shows that the dynasty lasted from around 1000 CE to 1343 CE.

The Hoysalas probably began as an extended family of indigenous hill-chiefs. Evidence found on an epigraph from the time of Narasimha III associates them with the Malapa tribe in the Western Ghats of Karnataka[1]. The king is given the title of *Malaparal ganda* (Champion among the Malapas).

The Hoysala area, comprising modern day Shimoga, Chikmagalur, Hassan and Coorg was known as Malnad, or Malenadu. However, epigraphic inscriptions have to be treated with caution. A 1229 CE inscription states that Narasimha II was ruling from Kanchipuram and that the ocean was his boundary. Prof Rangaraju of Mysore University suggests that this is "sheer exaggeration"[2].

Hoysala origins: reality and myth

Evidence from early Hoysala remains indicates that the dynasty originated in Sosevur (or Sosavir), where Sala, the first chieftain of the line supposedly killed a tiger to protect his guru, probably a Jain[3]. Prior to the conquest of Talakad in 1116 CE by the Hoysala ruler Vishnuvardhana, the Hoysalas appear to have ruled in this "underdeveloped forested and hilly region of the Western Ghats of present day Karnataka"[4]. Sosevur is today identified with Angadi in Mudigere Taluk of Chikmagalur District. Among the remains identified as Hoysala are five temples, two of them have been identified as Jain *basadis*, dating back to the 10th century. The three other temples are dedicated to Kesava, Patalarudreshwara and Mallikarjuna[5].

It has proved impossible to obtain any definitive evidence about the beginning of the Hoysala dynasty. The Sala myth is ubiquitous in Hoysala lands: many temples have carvings depicting Sala killing the tiger (fig 2).

But who was Sala?

It is not absolutely clear whether Sala was the same as Nripakama, or whether Sala actually existed or is simply an apocryphal story absorbed into the annals of Hoysala legend. Some evidence exists that the Hoysalas attempted to link their genealogy to that of the ancient Yadavas, the clan of the deity, Krishna, an avatar of Vishnu, claiming that they originated in Dwaraka in Gujarat, the town associated with Krishna. Narasimha III bore titles like *Yadava-kulambara - dyumani* (Sun in the sky of the Yadava Kula), identified on Hoysala inscriptions[6]. This would be entirely in keeping with the mediaeval Indian custom of legitimising the rule of powerful new monarchs by linking their genealogy to deities. An 1133 CE inscription from the Belur area claims a direct link between the Yadavas and Sala[7]. This inscription also ties in with the claim that the story of Sala and the tiger surfaced during the reign of Vishnuvardhana (1108-1142 CE) and that only then did the dynasty became associated with it[8].

From Brahma was Atri, from him was Soma, from him Pururava, from him Ayu, from him Nahusha, from him Yayati, from him Yadu, in whose line arose Sala. When for the increase of wealth of that King Sala's kingdom, a certain Jaina-batisa by his mantras was bringing the goddess Padmavati of Sasakapura into subjection, a tiger sprang forth upon them to break the spell, when Yogesvara, holding out the candle of his camara, said "poy Sala" (hit him Sala) on which he fearlessly smote it: from which time the name Poysala came to the Yadu kings, and the flag of a tiger waving on a rod…

3

THE HOYSALA DYNASTY

Sala (possibly same as) Nripakama

c.1000-1045 CE

Vinayaditya

c. 1045-1098 CE

Ereyanga

Ballala I

c.1100-1108 CE

Vishnuvardhana

c.1108-1142 CE

Narasimha I

c.1142-1173 CE

Ballala II

c.1173-1220 CE

Narasimha II

c.1220-1235 CE

Someshwara

c.1235-1354 CE

Narasimha III   Ramanatha

Kingdom partitioned

c.1253-92 CE

Ballala III

c.1292-1343 CE

c.1346 CE dynasty wiped out

Fig 3. The Hoysala Dynasty

The early Hoysalas are generally regarded as feudatories of the Later Chalukyas (of Kalyani). The word "feudatories" is problematic, having originally been applied to European cultures. Therefore it is justifiable to question its relevance to mediaeval India. Prof Ajay Sinha refers to the Hoysalas as "small chieftains under the ... Chalukyas of Kalyana" [9]. Whilst avoiding the word feudatories this does not clarify the relationship between the two dynasties. Other scholars prefer to regard mediaeval India in terms of segmentary states, implying perhaps a greater degree of autonomy than suggested by the term feudatory, the subordination being "largely symbolic" [10]. This, naturally, involved gifts to Brahmins and temples in return for kingly protection. Scholars also refer to *samantas* (Hindu princelings) whose territories are gradually integrated into the realm of a great ruler, thus creating an "Imperial kingdom" [11]. It is accepted that the Chalukyas originally held some sort of overlordship over the Hoysalas, and therefore the Hoysalas will, where appropriate in these chapters, be referred to as feudatories of the Chalukyas.

Fig 4 is a map of peninsular India, showing some of the major 12th-13th century dynasties. The Hoysala territory, along with several other minor kingdoms, was sandwiched between the Kalyani Chalukyas to the north and the Cholas to the south. During the course of the 12th century the Hoysalas would turn on their Chalukya overlords and eventually overcome them, as well as defeating the Cholas at Talakad.

Three branches of Chalukyas held sway over parts of Karnataka at various times during the mediaeval period. These were:

1. The Chalukyas of Badami, also known as the Early Chalukyas or the Western Chalukyas.

5

2. The Chalukyas of Vengi, also known as the Eastern Chalukyas. These were an offshoot of the Badami Chalukyas.

3. The Chalukyas of Kalyani (or Kalyana) also known as the Later Chalukyas or the Later Western Chalukyas.

Fig 4. Major 12ᵗʰ and 13ᵗʰ peninsular Indian dynasties

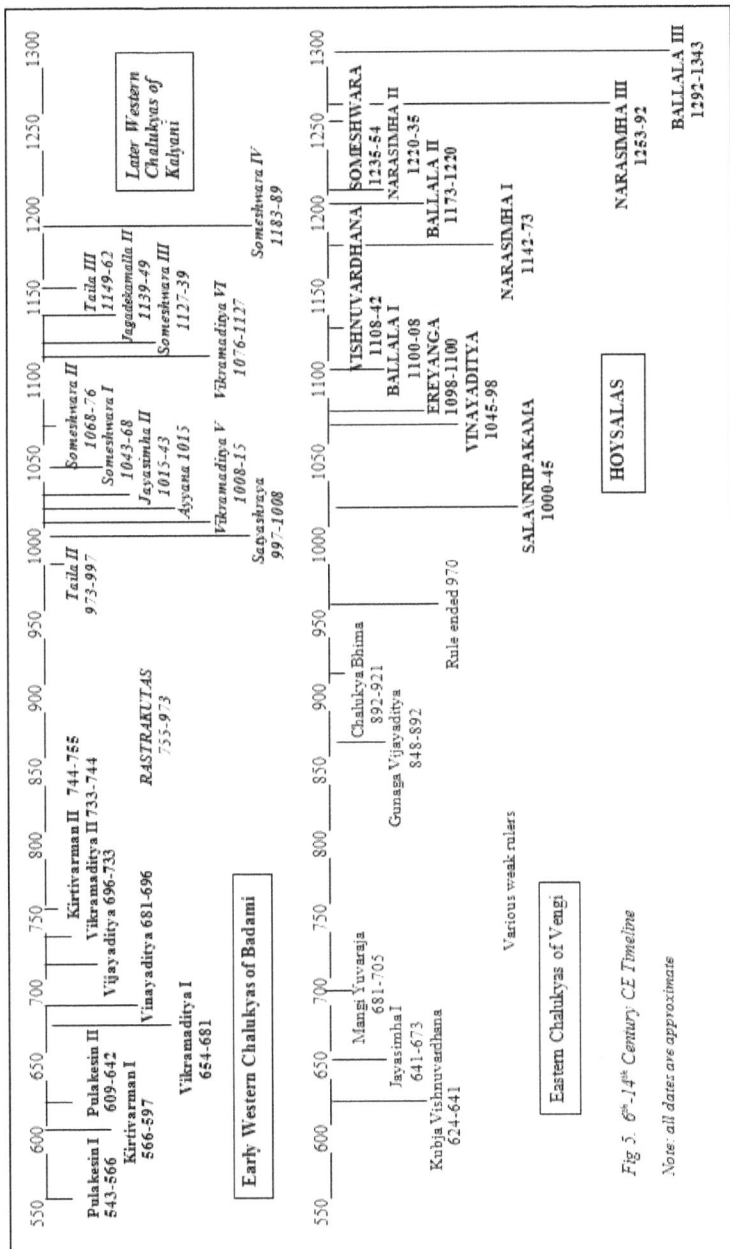

Early Western Chalukyas of Badami

Timeline (550–1300):

- Pulakesin I 543-566
- Kirtivarman I 566-597
- Pulakesin II 609-642
- Vikramaditya I 654-681
- Vinayaditya 681-696
- Vikramaditya II 696-733
- Kirtivarman II 733-744
- 744-755
- *RASTRAKUTAS 755-973*
- *Taila II 973-997*

Later Western Chalukyas of Kalyani

- Satyashraya 997-1008
- Vikramaditya V 1008-15
- Ayyana 1015
- Jayasimha II 1015-43
- Someshwara I 1043-68
- Someshwara II 1068-76
- Vikramaditya VI 1076-1127
- Someshwara III 1127-39
- Jagadekamalla II 1139-49
- Taila III 1149-62
- Someshwara IV 1183-89

Eastern Chalukyas of Vengi

- Kubja Vishnuvardhana 624-641
- Jayasimha I 641-673
- Mangi Yuvaraja 681-705
- Gunaga Vijayaditya 848-892
- Chalukya Bhima 892-921
- Various weak rulers
- Rule ended 970

HOYSALAS

- SALA/NRIPAKAMA 1000-45
- VINAYADITYA 1045-98
- EREYANGA 1098-1100
- BALLALA I 1100-08
- VISHNUVARDHANA 1108-42
- NARASIMHA I 1142-73
- BALLALA II 1173-1220
- NARASIMHA II 1220-35
- SOMESHWARA 1235-54
- NARASIMHA III 1253-92
- BALLALA III 1292-1343

Fig 5. 6th-14th Century CE Timeline

Note: all dates are approximate

The time-line in fig 5 shows all three Chalukya dynasties and the Hoysala dynasty. It can be seen that the dynasty contemporaneous with the Hoysalas was the Later Chalukya dynasty based in Kalyani.

The Hoysalas remained nominal feudatories of the Kalyani Chalukyas until 1192 CE when Ballala II ousted the last of them and proclaimed himself emperor. However, Ballala II was not the first powerful Hoysala king. Arguably the most important of the Hoysala monarchs was Vishnuvardhana. Besides initiating a revolt against the Chalukyas, his reign heralded an era in which some of the finest early temples, including the Chennakesava at Belur were built. The Hoysaleshwara in Halebid (Dorasamudra) was also started during his reign. Prior to the reign of Vishnuvardhana the Hoysalas had been Jains. It is thought that Vishnuvardhana, previously known as Bittiga, was converted to Vaishnavism by the great religious teacher Ramanuja during the latter's exile in Karnataka after he fled from Shaiva persecution in Tamil Nadu. However, no epigraphic evidence has been found to confirm this[12].

In the mid-13th century the kingdom was divided between two Hoysala brothers, resulting in weakness that lead to the eventual conquest of the northern Hoysala territory by the Yadavas (also known as the Seunas). For this reason subsequent temple building was restricted to areas around Hassan and Mysore, the heartland of the Hoysala dynasty. The temples at Govindanahalli, Belvadi, Hosaholalu and Somnathapur are regarded among the most important to be built during this time[13].

The Hoysalas dominated much of southern Karnataka during the 13th century, even taking parts of Chola territory in Tamil Nadu. However, at the beginning of the 14th century, the

Tughlak sultanate pressed southward from Delhi with the aim of conquering South India. The last Hoysala king, Ballala III, submitted to them in 1311 CE thus ending the independence of the Hoysala dynasty. However, until the death of Ballala III, the Hoysalas remained powerful and participated in revolts against the sultanate, particularly in the south. Indeed it was during such an action in Madurai that Ballala met his death *c.*1342/3 CE. The Hoysala dynasty was finally wiped out by the emergence of the Vijayanagara dynasty in the mid-14th century.

Chapter 2: Twelve Hoysala temple sites

The map in fig 6 shows the location, within the heartland of Hoysala territory, of the following twelve temples that form the basis of this book. Other temples built by the main Karnataka dynasties between 6th and 14th centuries are also shown on fig 6. The temples at these locations are as follows:

1. DODDAGADDUVALLI: the Lakshmidevi temple
2. BELUR: the Chennakesava temple
3. HALEBID: the Hoysaleshwara temple
4. MARLE: the Chennakesava and Siddeshwara twin temples
5. BELVADI: the Viranarayana temple
6. ARSIKERE: the Ishwara temple
7. GOVINDANAHALLI: the Panchalingeshwara temple
8. HOSAHOLALU: the Lakshminarayana temple
9. JAVAGAL: the Lakshminarasimha temple
10. HOSABUDNUR: the Ananthapadmanabha temple
11. SOMNATHAPUR: The Panchalingeshwara temple
12. SOMNATHAPUR: The Kesava temple

All the above temples are situated in present-day Karnataka Temples 1, 2 3, 6 and 9 are located in the Hassan District. Temples 4 and 5 are in the Chikmagalur District, Temples 7, 8 and 10 in the Mandya District, and temples 11 & 12 are in the Mysore District.

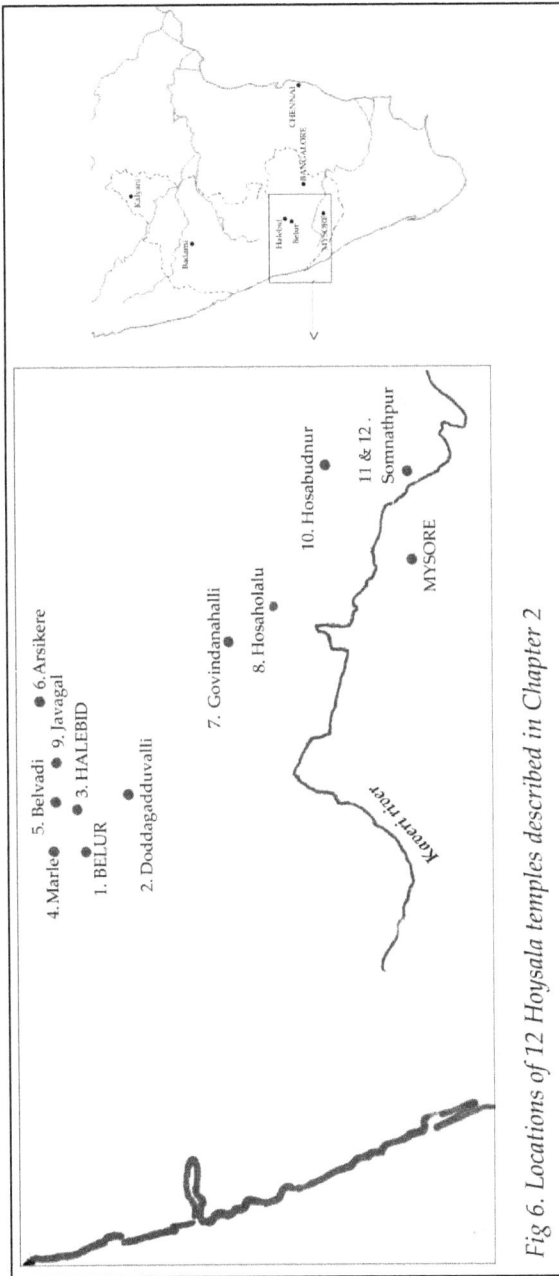

Fig 6. Locations of 12 Hoysala temples described in Chapter 2

1. The Lakshmidevi temple at Doddagadduvalli
(Figs 7a and 7b))

This temple, in an isolated village in the Hassan district of Karnataka, was constructed in 1113 or 1114 CE during the reign of Vishnuvardhana and his Jain wife, Shantala Devi. The patrons were the merchant Kullahana Rahuta and his wife Sahaja Devi. It is the earliest temple of the twelve in this study and one of the earliest to display some distinctly Hoysala characteristics. It is a *caturkuta*, a temple consisting of four *garbhagrihas*, possibly the only one built by the Hoysalas. The four main shrines face north, south, east and west and are dedicated to Kali, Vishnu, Lakshmi and Bhuthanatha Linga respectively. However, it also has five additional shrines, one freestanding dedicated to Bhairava and the other four embedded into the corners of the *prakara* wall. An inscription of 1113 refers to it as "the temple of Goddess Mahalakshmi" showing that the temple was always dedicated to Lakshmi and was not renamed at a later date[14]. It is particularly unusual for the main deity in a syncretic temple (ie one that is a blend of both Vishnu and Shiva traditions) to be Vaishnava.

All the shrine superstructures except the eastern (Lakshmi) shrine are in a hybrid style known as *Phamsana*. The pyramidal Dravida structure is maintained, but consists only of tooth-like horizontal rows. It is related to the *Kalinga* style of architecture prevalent in Orissa.

Fig 7a. Doddagaduvalli: Lakshmidevi temple from the north-west

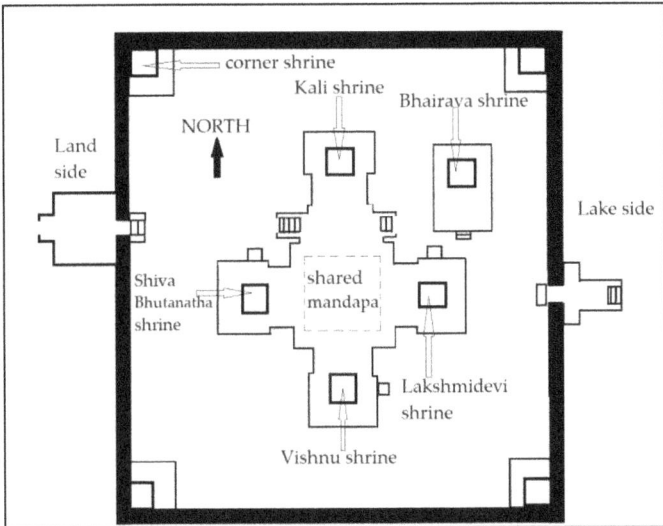

Fig 7b. Doddagaduvalli: Lakshmidevi temple plan

2. The Chennakesava temple at Belur (Figs 8a and 8b)

According to epigraphic evidence the Chennakesava was established in 1117 CE by the Hoysala ruler, Vishnuvardhana, after a victory over the Cholas[15]. Belur, situated in the Hassan district of southern Karnataka, was the capital of the Hoysala Kingdom in its initial stages.

The Chennakesava is an *ekakuta* temple, that is, having only one *vimana*. It has features reminiscent of some temples in Maharashtra, which Vishnuvardhana's father could have encountered after a notable Hoysala military victory over the Pramara king Jayasimha of Malava. Possibly the Hoysalas wanted to make an imperial statement, a new creation and experiment with a variety of sources, resulting in many innovations and hallmarks subsequently identified with the Hoysala "style"[16].

Unfortunately it is an incomplete temple, having lost its superstructure. A 1298 CE inscription refers to its restoration due to rotten wood and fallen bricks, implying that the original *shikhara* was constructed from bricks and mortar[17.] It is possible that there were originally five *talas*[18]. Repeated attempts were made to restore some kind of a plausiblt tower, but these were finally abandoned in the nineteenth century since when it has been left with a flat roof.

The quality of the Chennakesava carvings are regarded as unsurpassed in the whole of Hoysala temple art. The temple took 103 years to complete and is one of the greatest Hoysala masterpieces.

Fig 8a. Belur: Chennakesava temple viewed from the west

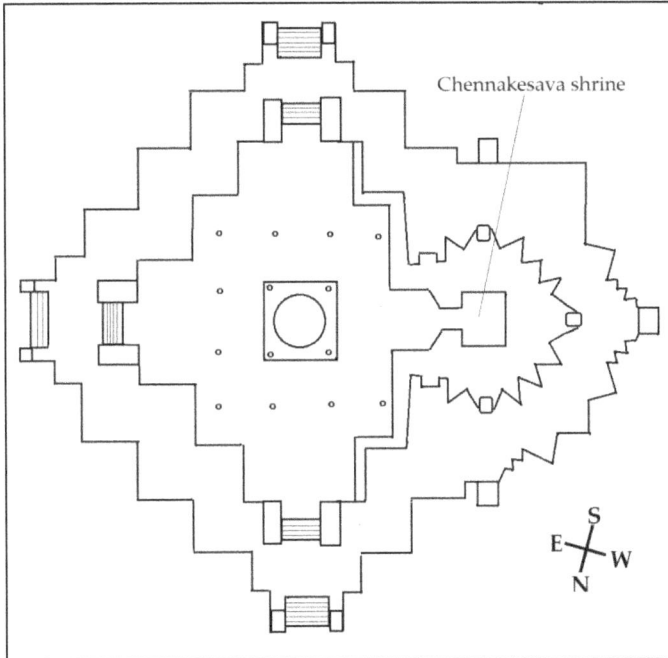

Fig 8b. Simplified plan of the Chennakesava temple

3. The Hoysaleshwara temple at Halebid
(Figs 9a and 9b)

Following the construction of the Chennakesava temple in Belur, the construction of an equally impressive Shaiva temple appears to have been a necessity. Halebid, known by the Hoysalas as Dorasamudra, was the Hoysala capital after independence from the Later Chalukyas.

There is no inscription that records the dedication of the Hoysaleshwara, but a nearby inscription of 1121 CE refers to a temple in Dorasamudra constructed by a commander-in-chief named Ketamalla in about 1120 CE for Vishnuvardhana[19]. It was evidently completed by the architect Kedaroja between 1141 CE and 1160 CE during the reign of Narasimha I[20]. The extent of this completion is a matter of debate. The two *vimana* superstructures of this *dvikuta* temple are missing. It is not known whether, for some reason, they were never built[21], or whether the Hoysaleshwara originally had brick and mortar towers, which no longer exist[22]. To add to the debate, a 1990 survey of the dried up Dorasamudra lake suggests that its embankments may have come from the *shikharas* of the Hoysaleshwara temple[23].

Despite the missing superstructure the Hoysaleshwara is regarded as one of the most spectacular monuments in India, possibly in the world. At the time of writing it is, along with the Chennakesava at Belur, on the UNESCO World Heritage Site tentative list.

Fig 9a. Halebid: Hoysaleshwara temple showing the two vimanas

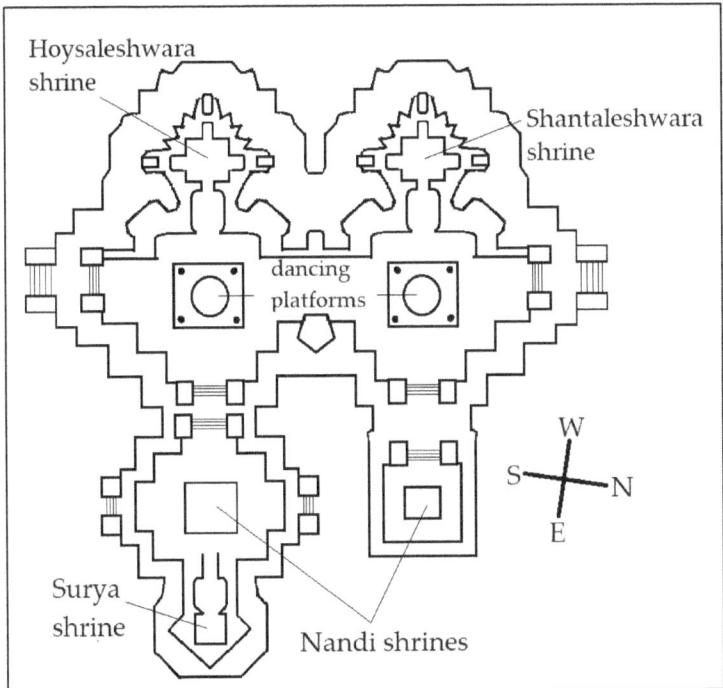

Fig 9b. Hoysaleshwara temple plan

4. The Chennakesava and Siddeshwara temples, Marle (Figs 10a, 10b and 10c)

These two side-by-side soapstone temples, amount to a syncretic temple with two independent shrines, dedicated to Chennakesava and Siddeshwara. They are situated in the tiny 'off the beaten track' village of Marle (Mirale, Marale) some twelve kilometres from Chickmagalur. This temple complex has inconclusive dating: neither Hardy nor Foekema have dated it and it has been largely neglected by other scholars. It has been suggested that the elaborate 3 ½ metre high stele between the temples, giving details of the history of their construction, confirms that they were both constructed during the region of Vishnuvardhana and that the village was previously called Vishnuvardhana Kesava *agrahara*[24]. The works of two of the foremost authorities in the field of Hoysala architecture illustrate the uncertainty over these temples. Both Prof Adam Hardy's[25] and Prof S Settar's[26] descriptions of the two shrines contain some ambiguities regarding the identity of each temple. Dr. Gerard Foekema's description is clearer and in accord with what I have observed at the site and therefore will be taken as authoritative[27]

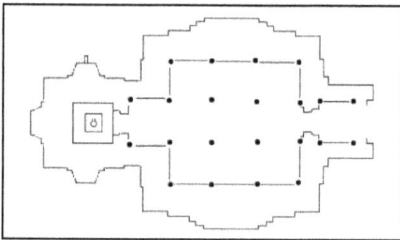

Fig 10a. Plan of the Siddeshwara temple

Fig 10b. Marle: Chennakesava and Siddeshwara temples

Figs 10c. Marle: Chennakesava and Siddeshwara temples

19

5. The Viranarayana temple at Belvadi (figs 11a, 11b and 11c)

Belvadi is situated on the road between Javagal and Chikmagalur and has a Hoysala soapstone temple, which boasts what Foekema regards as "the most majestic temple front in all Hoysala architecture"[28.]

The Viranarayana temple was constructed in two phases and there are distinct differences between the first and the second phase. The newer part of the temple is based on an extraordinary plan. The origins of this temple have not been as well documented as the more familiar temples, but it is known to have been constructed during the later part of the 12th century[29]. Originally an *ekakuta* (single shrine) temple with a *vimana* on the western side dedicated to Viranarayana, it was extended, possibly at the beginning of the 13th century, into a *trikuta* (three shrines) temple with the addition of a massive open hall with two *vimanas* leading off it to the north and south. All three *vimanas* are dedicated to forms of Vishnu.

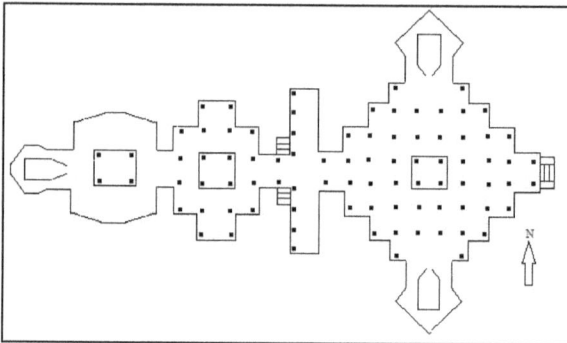

Fig 11a. Belvadi: Plan of Viranarayana temple

Fig 11b. Belvadi: Viranarayana temple showing the two later vimanas and open mandapa.

Fig 11c. Belvadi: Viranarayana temple showing earlier vimana and mandapa, linking corridor and side entrance

6. The Ishwara temple at Arsikere (figs 12a and 12b Also see fig 15c)

Arsikere is a small town some thirty-two kilometres northeast of Halebid. In medieval India it was on the main trade route from Kanchi in the east to the vicinity around present day Mangalore on the west coast.

Along with Belur and Dorasamudra, Arsikere occupied a commanding place on the route down to the south from Devaragiri and Kalyani. The town was a centre for the horse breeding and trading in elephants, gemstones and farming products such as maize, sugar, mangoes and turmeric. Therefore it was a town of considerable wealth and importance. Arsikere has been described as the southern Aihole[30].

According to epigraphic evidence, the Ishwara temple was built in 1220 CE, which places it during reign of Ballala II[31]. It is an *ekakuta* soapstone temple, constructed on an east-west axis, one of the most complex and idiosyncratic of all Hoysala temples in plan and form, with a spectacular open *mandapa*.

This gorgeous temple is a hidden Hoysala gem and well worth the effort of making a detour from the better-known temple sites in the region. Its harmonious appearance belies the extreme sophistication of its design.

Fig 12a. Arsikere: Ishwara temple. L to R vimana, closed mandapa, open mandapa

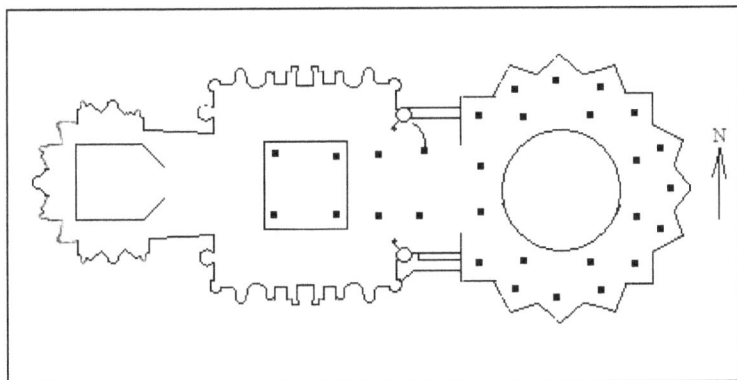

Fig 12b. Arsikere: Ishwara temple plan.

7. The Panchalingeshwara temple at Govindanahalli (figs 13a and 13b)

The isolated village of Govindanahalli in the Krishnarajpet Taluk of the Mandya District of Karnataka harbours a large Hoysala *panchalingeshwara* (five shrines) temple. It is one of only two remaining Hoysala *panchalingeshwara* temples. Its precise date of construction is unknown, but an estimate can be made from clues left by inscriptions. An inscription in the *navaranga* is dated *Saka* 1159 (1236 CE). It refers to the founding of an *agrahara* and suggests that the temple was built as part of this plan. If nothing else, it appears to confirm that the temple was already in existence in 1236 CE. Another clue is given by the *dvarapalas* guarding the temple entrances. Two of these bear the name of Mallitamma, the sculptor overwhelmingly associated with the Kesava temple in Somnathapur. The date of around 1230 CE has been suggested on the assumption that this is an early work by Mallitamma as the sculpture is immature[32]. Collyer, however, suggests a date circa 1250 CE, which implies that the *navaranga* inscription was earlier and later placed in the temple[33]. Five *Shivalingas* are installed in the five sanctuaries, each of which has its own superstructure.

From the temple's plan it can be seen that the fifth (northern) shrine lacks the three *ankanas* (squares) that separate its *navaranga* from that of the fourth shrine. It follows that this last *vimana* is unevenly spaced. In addition, the two entrances are not placed symmetrically when the whole temple is considered. If, however, the fifth *vimana* is removed the remaining four create a perfectly symmetrical temple. The fifth *vimana* may have been a later addition. However, the eminent Hoysala scholar, Foekema suggests that it may originally have been a four-shrine temple[34]. If this is correct, the Lakshmidevi temple at Doddagadduvalli is not, after all, the only *caturkuta* temple built by the Hoysalas. He noted, however, that the fifth shrine is so similar to the other four that it is nearly as old. There has been some poor restoration work carried out on this temple. This could conceivably have "muddied the waters" regarding accurate dating.

Fig 13a. Govindanahalli: Panchalingeshwara temple

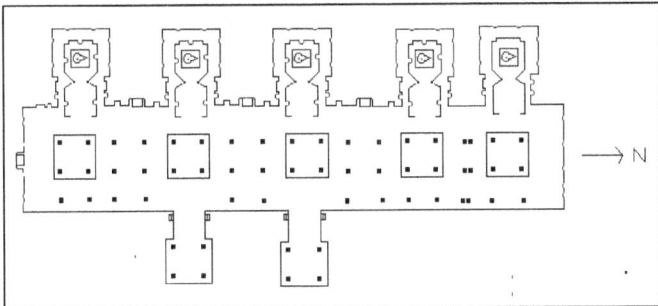

Fig 13b. Govindanahalli: Panchalingeshwara temple plan

8. The Lakshminarayana temple in Hosaholalu (figs 14a, 14b and 14c.)

The Archives of the American Institute of Indian studies suggest that the Lakshminarayana temple in Hosaholalu was probably constructed in around 1240 CE[35]. At that time Hosaholalu was a prosperous *agrahara* with Shaiva and Jain as well as Vaishnava associations. It is a *trikuta* soapstone temple with a lateral northern shrine to Lakshminarasimha and a southern one to Venugopala. The central Lakshminarayana shrine faces east. Despite an unsympathetic later addition it is a beautiful temple and well worth a visit, which can easily be combined with the Panchalingeshwara temple at Govindanahalli.

Fig 14a. Hosaholalu: Lakshminarayana temple from the west

Fig 14b. Hosaholalu Lakshminarayana temple from the South

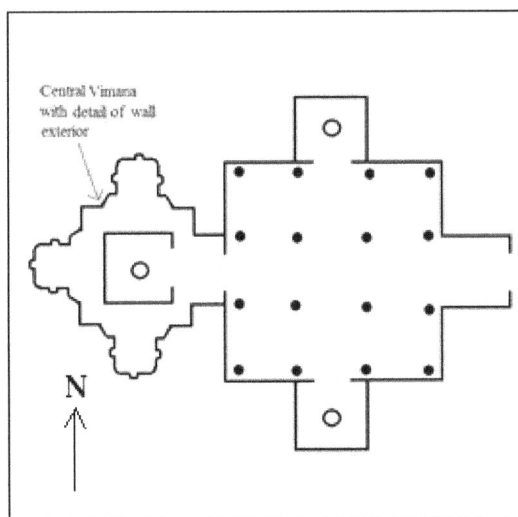

Fig 14c. Hosaholalu: Lakshminarayana temple plan

9. The Lakshminarasimha temple at Javagal (figs 15a, 15b and 15c)

The village of Javagal, some fifteen kilometres from Halebid, and 25 km from Arsikere, is home to a 13th century *trikuta* Hoysala soapstone temple dedicated to Lakshminarasimha. It has three equally–sized shrines and was probably constructed in around 1250 CE [36]. Lakshminarasimha (Vishnu as his avatar Narasimha, the man-lion, with his consort, Lakshmi) is found in the northern lateral shrine, not the central shrine. The southern shrine houses Venugopala. The main *garbhagriha* is dedicated to Sridhara, another form of Vishnu. This arrangement is not unusual in a Lakshminarasimha temple[37].

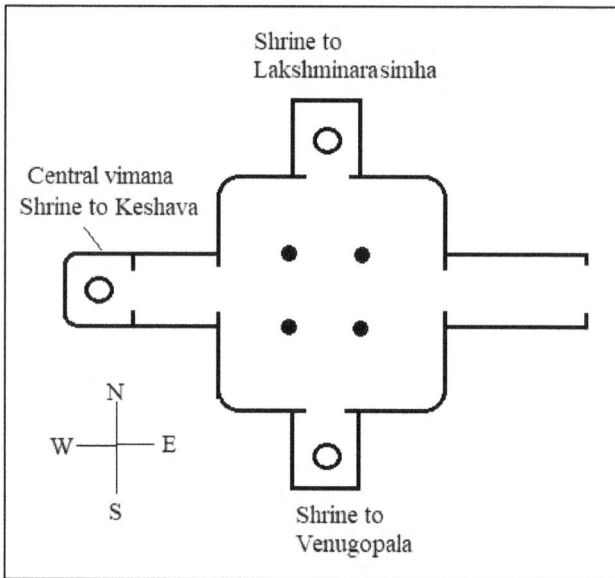

Fig 15a. Javagal:, simplified Lakshminarasimha temple plan

Fig 15b. Javagal: Lakshminarasimha temple

Fig 15c. The road between Javagal and Arsikere

10. The Ananthapadmanabha temple at Hosabudnur (fig 16a and 16b)

Today Hosabudnur is a tiny village near Mandya just off the Mysore-Bangalore road. Two major temples were constructed there during the Hoysala era, the Kasivisveshwara temple and the Ananthapadmanabha. While the former has been allowed to fall into even greater decay the latter has been carefully restored.

An inscription of 1276 CE indicates that the village was made into an *agrahara*[38]. Although it does not state the date of construction of the Ananthapadmanabha temple it is likely that it was constructed during this period, i.e. during the reign of Narasimha III. Stylistically it could be dated to around 1260 CE.[39] A plaque on the site, erected after the recent restoration, gives a date of 1269 CE, which would make it exactly contemporaneous with the two temples in Somnathapur.

This soapstone *ekakuta* temple was restored between 1994 when Gerard Foekema reported it in a ruined state[40], and 1998 when Dr N S Rangaraju of Mysore University reported restoration completed[41]. Fig 16a shows the temple after restoration. Even before restoration the *vimana* was intact. The plaque indicates that the whole temple was disassembled and rebuilt. However, the *vimana* has been accurately reassembled, suggesting that care was taken to ensure the authenticity of as much of the remainder as possible.

Fig 16a. Hosabudnur: Ananthapadmanabha temple

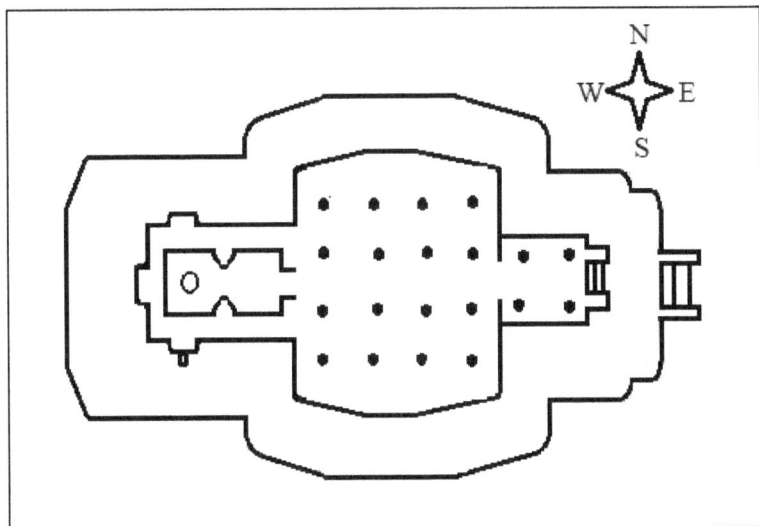

Fig 16b. Ananthapadmanabha temple plan

11. The Panchalingeshwara temple at Somnathapur (figs 17a, 17b and 17c)

The granite Panchalingeshwara temple at Somnathapur is situated slightly southeast of the Kesava temple, set back across fields, and half-concealed by shrubbery. There are now only three *vimanas* left standing and much of the *navaranga* has also disappeared. At the side of the temple is a very fine soapstone stele (see Fig 17c). Inscriptions date this temple to around 1268 CE, and indicate that the patron, like that of the Kesava temple, was Somanatha. This and the one at Govindanahalli are the only two remaining Hoysala *panchalingeshwara* temples, though inscriptions identify eight[42].

Fig 17a. Somnathpur: Panchalingeshwara temple

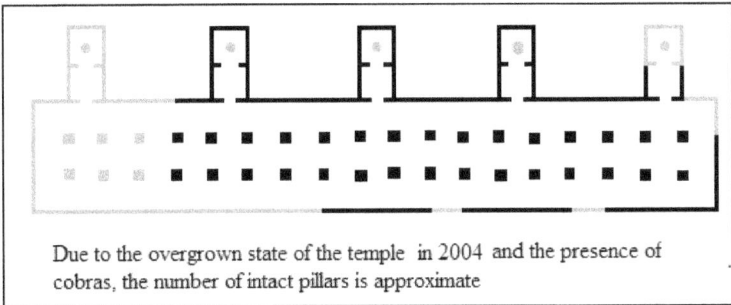

Due to the overgrown state of the temple in 2004 and the presence of cobras, the number of intact pillars is approximate

Fig 17b. Somnathapur: Panchalingeshwara temple plan.

Fig 17c. Somnathapur: Hoysala Stele outside the Panchalingeshwara temple.

12. The Kesava temple at Somnathapur (figs 18a and 18b)

The Kesava temple was built during the reign of Narasimha III. It was the last great temple to be built during the Hoysala period, and one of the three greatest, and certainly one of the loveliest, ever to be built under this dynasty. It is one of the few complete and relatively unrestored Hoysala temples existing today. A great deal is known about its construction because there are many inscriptions. It was completed in 1268/9 CE. Like the majority of Hoysala temples, it is not a Royal temple but was built under the patronage of a high-ranking minister, General Somanatha, who was also a relative of Narasimha III. Somanatha created an *agrahara* from an existing village which he then renamed Somnathapur after himself. In keeping with Vaishnava tradition, the Kesava was constructed in the centre of this village. Under Narasimha III forty-three Vaishnava temples received patronage, of which twenty-nine were newly created. Although the king was not involved in founding these new centres he was still the source of all major temple construction projects because of his endowments. Most lavish was his endowment to Somnathapur to enable Somanatha to establish the Kesava temple. Therefore it owes as much to Narasimha as it does to Somanatha.

The endowment Narasimha made yielded an annual income of 3500 *gadyanas*. A grant to the Kesava in 1268 CE was the largest made by any mediaeval king of the lower Deccan[43]. The *trikuta* temple is built of soapstone, which is found in the areas around Halebid and Belur but is not natural to the area around Somnathapur. The fact that this luxury stone was imported into the area for the purposes of building the Kesava temple is testimony to its wealth and importance.

Fig 18a. Somnathapur: the Kesava temple

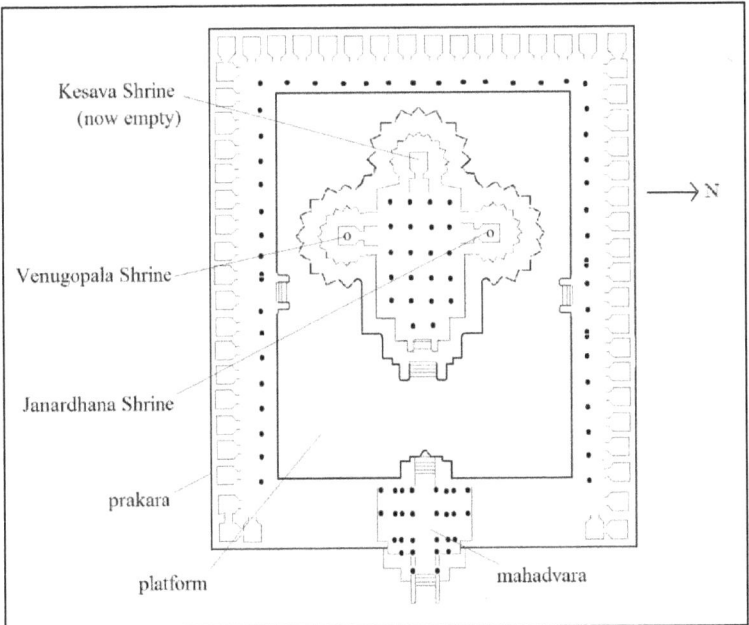

Kesava Shrine
(now empty)

Venugopala Shrine

Janardhana Shrine

prakara

platform

mahadvara

→ N

Fig 18b. Somnathapur: Kesava temple plan

Chapter 3: Dancing temples: the forms and plans of Hoysala vimanas

Reaching for the stars: the plan

The stellate plan is regarded as one of the hallmarks of Hoysala temples. A stellate appearance does not necessarily mean that the temple plan is a full star. Sometimes an orthogonal or "mixed" plan can achieve a "star-like" appearance due to the complexity and staggering of aedicules. Fig 19a shows the principle of the sixteen-point star (*sodasasra*[44]) plan favoured by the Hoysalas. The plan is still based on the square, the most important Hindu symbol of the universe, and the basis of the *vastumandala*. To create the star shape the square is rotated four times in equal steps of 22 ½ degrees. It can also be seen as four superimposed rotated squares. Despite its now almost circular appearance it can still be described in terms of its originating square. This is important when considering its aedicular structure. A mix of star and square is sometimes called a half star as in fig 19b.[45].

The different plans are not always easily distinguishable and have caused confusion in writing on Hoysala temples. This confusion is exemplified by the Chennakesava temple in Belur. It has points on two different sizes and some oblong sections. The Hoysaleshwara temple in Halebid has a similar plan. This has led Del Bonta to dismiss the possibility of an iconographic reason for using a particular star plan, the Chennakesava being a Vaishnava and the Hoysaleshwara a Shaiva temple[46].

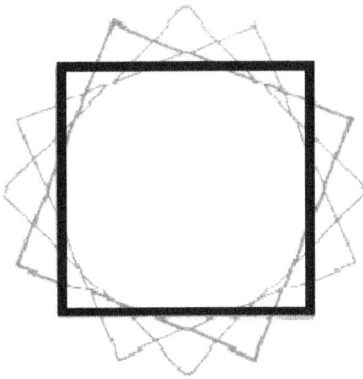

Fig 19a. A sixteen-point full star plan formed by rotating a square.

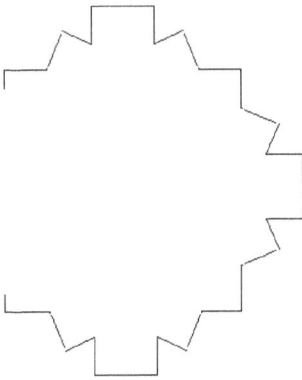

Fig 19b A half-star plan.

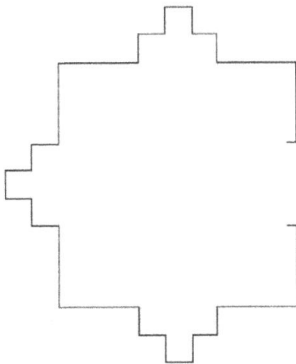

Fig 19c. A simple square plan.

The mix can be seen quite clearly in the shrine walls in figs 8b and 9b. Del Bonta, citing Judith Patt, calls both plans twenty-point stars[47]. Hardy describes both temples as stellate (as opposed to semi-stellate) *vimanas* based on sixteen points, with huge cardinal orthogonal wall-shrines, (which presumably disguise their fully stellate form)[48]. Foekema similarly describes the plans of these two temples as sixteen-point stars where the central points have been replaced by four sections, which push apart the intermediate points. However, he calls of this type of plan a *pancharatha* half star plan[49].

Simply stated, if the walls of the *vimana* are simply pushed out so that they remain parallel with the original square then it is a square *vimana* as in fig 19c. If some of them are not parallel to the original square it is a half star as in fig 19b. If none of them are parallel, so that all the aedicules between the corners have not simply been pushed out but rotated the result is a full star as in fig 19a.

Foekema mentions three Later Chalukya temples as having a stellate plan, the Doddabasappa temple in Dambal (fig 20) and earlier ones at Savadi and Konnur. He does not, however, consider any of these as forerunners of Hoysala temples, two being too old and therefore not related in a direct line and the third - the Dambal temple - being a twenty-four point star, unrelated to the sixteen-point plan favoured by the Hoysalas[50]. The Savadi temple does have sixteen points but Foekema maintains that it is unconnected to the Hoysala star temples, since the first Hoysala star, the Chennakesava in Belur, has points of two sizes and oblongs replacing some points (figs 8a and 8b).

In the opinion of at least one art historian, Settar, the Doddabasappa temple is unsurpassed by any Hoysala work[51]. Others would disagree.

Fig 20. Twenty-four point vimana: Doddabasappa temple in Dambal

Settar suggests that the Hoysalas' main contribution to the stellate plan is "their ability to elaborate, and to amalgamate the two forms of the stellate plan, of broken squares and broken circles"

The main architectural emphasis of the Lakshminarayana temple in Hosaholalu is placed on the central *vimana,* which is the only one to have a half star plan, a combination of right angles and acute angles based on a sixteen-point star[52]. This is partly shown in fig 14a. The two lateral *vimanas* are based on a square plan. The original western *vimana* of the Viranarayana temple at Belvadi (fig 11a) has an orthogonal plan. For the second phase a large open *mandapa* was added to the east. Leading off from it are a southern *vimana* dedicated to Venugopala, a staggered square with three projections on each side (a *triratha*) and a half star northern *vimana* dedicated to Yoga Narasimha, likewise a *triratha* This *vimana* may be the earliest Hoysala semi-stellate *vimana*[53]. The original Viranarayana shrine is now at the back. The *vimana* of the Ishwara temple at Arsikere is based on a sixteen-point star plan, which is shown in fig 12b. It is regarded as the "most varied one in Hoysala architecture and, consequently, in all Dravida architecture"[54] and will be considered further in conjunction with its form.

Into orbit: temple forms

The plan is the outline upon which the temple form is raised. It is therefore impossible to discuss one without considering its effects on the other. There has been constant debate about whether the Hoysala development of the stellate plan triggered a new temple form, or whether it facilitated evolution of a traditional Karnataka *vimana*, frequently referred to as Vesara.

The 12th century *Kamikagama* was one of the first southern texts to use the term Vesara. It is a Sanskrit word, which can be translated as "mule". This has led to the commonly held belief that Vesara temples were an amalgamation of Nagara and Dravida architecture. However, the *Kamikagama* usage may be too ambiguous to make a meaningful contribution to the debate. A theory that though Vesara had occasional northern overtones it had nothing that could be called a typical Nagara feature[55] has been dismissed by South Asian art historian A J Sinha as tentative[56]. Sinha maintains that Vesara did not break entirely new ground, however, a conceptual shift within the regional framework occurred disrupting a smooth, systematic flow in chronological terms. Nagara and Dravida continue to function separately in Vesara. He argues that Vesara cannot be understood as a synthesis of forms or of the continuation of Dravida. He sees the Vesara as a "regional modality of responding to the architectural world of the 11th century"[57].

Hardy sees smooth continuity of Dravida temple building from the time of the Early Chalukyas through to the Hoysala era. He prefers the term Karnata Dravida to describe these temples in preference to Vesara because it is "truer to the uninterrupted use of southern forms as the essential compositional elements, and to the continuity of transformation which takes place"[58]. He argues that these temples' northern characteristics are not due to an attempt to borrow from the north in order to create a hybrid temple, but because Karnata Dravida and Nagara simply developed in the same way. The changing temple form is the natural evolution of Dravida architecture in terms of its symbolic function, a tangible expression of the infinite.

The use of the term Vesara to describe whole temples was introduced by modern scholars[59]. Ancient southern texts only referred to some closing *kuta* roof shapes as Vesara. The *Isanasivagurudevapaddhati*, a mediaeval southern text, applies the distinction between Nagara, Dravida and Vesara to the *Ksudra-alpa-Vimanas* (the top of the temple) only[60]. In Later Chalukya and Hoysala architecture the direction of sunlight coupled with prolific decoration can change the perception of the *vimana*, wrongly suggesting a hybridisation between the dominating vertical lines of Nagara architecture and the horizontal lines of Dravida. Like Hardy, Foekema implies that the term Vesara is misleading because it suggests a non-existent category and obscures the Dravida character of temples[61]. Fig 21a shows the superstructure of the *vimanas* of the Kesava temple at Somnathapur. This view demonstrates how its verticality has led to theories of Nagara influence. The "stepped" pyramidal appearance of the Dravida *vimana* tower has given way to a much smoother outline, which could be construed as curvilinear. However, detailed analysis of the whole *vimana* structure, not simply the superstructure, casts doubt on such an assumption.

Fig 21a Somnathapur Keshava temple vimana superstructures

Fig 21b shows that although the towers have retained a horizontal alignment, they have also, in comparison with earlier temples, acquired a vertical alignment in keeping with the star points of the wall below, which arise from the *sodasasra* plan. In fact if the prominent *chadya* canopy separating the wall from the tower, and the second smaller canopy partway up the wall were removed, there would be no break in the vertical lines radiating from the top of the tower to the base of the wall. The stellate form is carried through from the plan to the dome at the top of the *vimana*, therefore giving it a ribbed shape reminiscent of the northern *amalaka*.

All three towers are very intricately ornamented and, in addition, the traditional Dravida components are virtually unrecognisable. In place of these there appear to be compressed rows of vertical slabs carved with *nasis* highly ornamented with floral patterns. However, fig 22, showing a section of the western *vimana* superstructure, shows that it is composed entirely of Dravida *kuta* aedicules. *Yakshas* emerge from the depth of the tower between pairs of pilasters representing miniature buildings.

Fig 21b. Somnathapur, Kesava: verticality and horizontality of the northern vimana

Fig 22. Somnathapur, Kesava: section of the western vimana

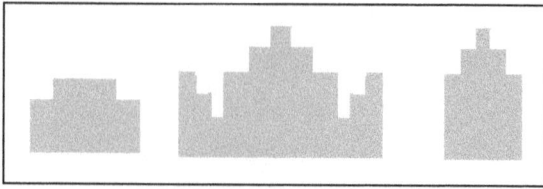

Fig 23. Schematic roof elements. Left to right: kuta, shala, panjara.[62]

Foekema suggests that many Hoysala temples only have schematic representation of the traditional Dravida pavilions that make up the roof. These amount to nothing more than indented slabs suggesting the roof outlines. This scheme is shown in fig 23[63].

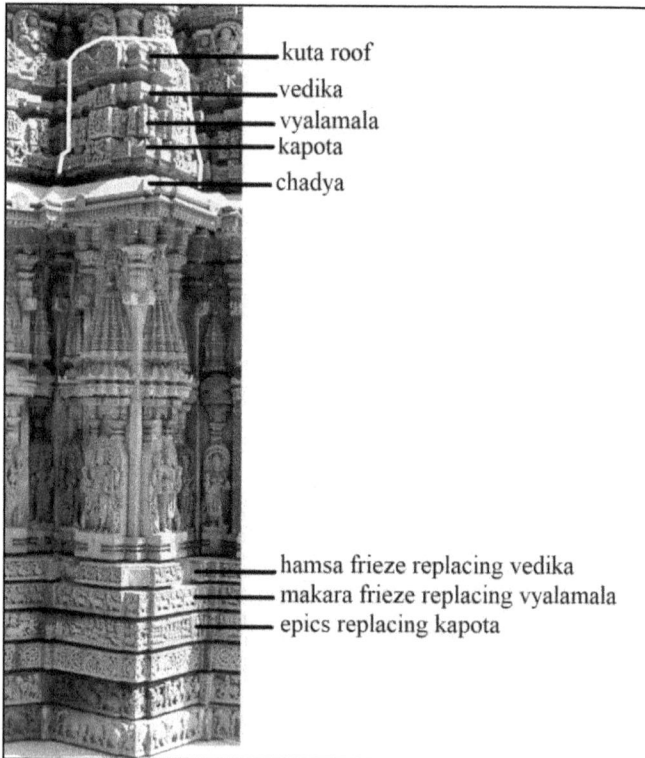

Fig 24a. Somnathapur, Kesava: kuta- aedicule

A *kuta* aedicule of the northern *vimana* of the Kesava can be seen in Fig 24a. The upper mouldings above the projecting *chadya* are composed of a *kapota*, a *vyalamala* and a *vedi* (*vedika*). The base mouldings have become a series of six intricately carved friezes running along the whole of the base of the back part of the temple. However, in the earlier Hoysaleshwara temple in Halebid, the transformation of the upper friezes at least can be shown to relate to Dravida mouldings (figs 24b & c). This will be discussed further in the next chapter.

Fig 24b. Halebid, Hoysaleshwara: Joist ends related to vyalamala visible beneath the makara frieze.

Fig 24c. Halebid, Hoysaleshwara: kapota shape discernible behind epic frieze

The Ishwara temple at Arsikere presents even more complexity. The star *vimana* has *stambha* aedicules, which are a feature of Nagara temples. The base mouldings include a *kumbha* moulding, which is only normally seen in Nagara temples (fig 25).

This is the only known example of a *kumbha* in a Dravida setting[64]. However, analysis of the whole elevation confirms that this is not a Nagara, but a five *tala* Dravida *vimana* including a closing *vedika* and *kuta* roof. Fig 26 shows four of the aedicules of one "side of the square" outlined.

The corner aedicules of each side are eight-pointed *kuta-stambhas*. Unusually, the *shala* aedicules are intermediate and have *kuta-stambhas* projecting from them. The central aedicules on each side are *kuta-stambhas*.

kuta roof

vedika (vedi)

vvalamala

kapota

chadya

vedika

vyalamala

kapota

kumuda

kumbha

Fig 25. Aedicule at Ishwara temple, Arsikere

8-pointed kuta-stambha   shala & kuta-stambha   kuta-stambha

Fig 26. Arsikere, Ishwara: aedicular structure of the vimana

Hardy describes the Ishwara *vimana* as an *astrabhadra*, meaning it has eight *bhadras* or principal projections, which are normally situated at the eight cardinal points[65]. However, in the case of the Ishwara, the principal projections are the intermediate ones, the combined *shala plus kuta-stambha* aedicules. Hardy interprets these and the stellate *kuta-stambhas* as unfurling "along their own orthogonal axes", while the centrally placed *kuta-stambha* aedicules orbit around the *vimana*. This arrangement, suggests Hardy, greatly increases the dynamism and sense of rotation. However, the projections equally manage to fuse together in perfect harmony. The result is a sense of of unity and fragmentation. It is this author's contention that dynamic fusion is equally present in the regular stellate Kesava temple at Somnathapur.

The stellate form was predominantly a Hoysala feature, occurring in only a few temples of the Later Chalukyas. This would suggest that either the Vesara/Karnata Dravida temple is also predominantly Hoysala, or that it is not dependent upon the stellate plan.

To this end it will be useful to compare the northern and southern *vimanas* of the Viranarayana temple at Belvadi (figs 27a & b). The southern, staggered square *vimana* is very slightly larger than the northern one, but the semi-stellate northern one is far more crowded with ornamentation due to the extra angles created by the star shape. This also creates greater verticality than on the southern *vimana*, and affects the Dravida appearance of the superstructure. However, there is no doubt that the articulation of all three *talas* is completely Dravida, the elements having been largely reduced to schematic structures and obscured by decoration.

Although the semi-stellate plan of the northern *vimana* accentuates the vertical curvilinear look, the features identified above as suggesting Nagara influence are all present in the southern *vimana*: the schematic *shalas* and *kutas*, compressed horizontal *haras*, ornamentation and some degree of verticality. Although this *vimana* is not stellate or semi-stellate, it does have a staggered/broken square plan. Therefore a staggered square plan can produce a curvilinear Vesara look. However, a stellate plan enhances this further.

Fig 27a. The Viranarayana temple at Belvadi: the southern (staggered square) vimana

Fig 27b. The Viranarayana temple at Belvadi The northern star vimana

It can be concluded that the Vesara temple is, architecturally, a completely Dravida structure. This can be seen by considering the *vimana* as a whole, rather than simply looking at the superstructure. The illusion of Nagara influence, particularly on the superstructure, has been created by the following:

1. Reduction of architectural components (*shalas* and *kutas)* to schematic elements.
2. Compressing of the horizontal planes, so that the pilasters of the aedicules in the upper storeys are foreshortened and sometimes disappear completely.
3. Extensive and elaborate decoration that obscures much of the remaining architectural articulation.
4. The stellate or broken square plan that carries through to the roof creating the sense of verticality associated with Nagara architecture. In some temples the resulting projections in the wall create wide central *bhadras* with niches (the width of the *garbhagriha*) representing the sanctum space. These are examples of Sinha's conceptual shift.

These features add up to an impression of increased verticality and a curvilinear outline, whilst remaining completely Dravida in form. Therefore Hardy's term Karnata Dravida is more valid than the term Vesara. The Hoysalas developed, but did not initiate the Karnata Dravida temple.

Hoysala stellate plans did not necessarily result in Dravida temples. Evidence indicates that the Chennakesava temple in Belur is a Nagara temple. Its aedicules are Nagara: they have a *shikhara,* a *kapota*, a *chadya,* and a *stambha*-type body (ie an aedicule whose body is a single, frequently staggered pillar, not a wall space between two pilasters). This rests on a *kapota*-topped pedestal. The pedestal has more sections than the Dravida pedestal, including a *kumbha* (See fig 28). In addition an early 20th century photograph by Cousens shows the temple with a Nagara *Bhumija mulaprasada*, albeit one dating from the 18th century. It is possible that some Nagara specialists migrated south into Hoysala territory. Adam Hardy attributes the designation Nagara to the similarity of the moulding shapes to those of Nagara temples in northern Karnataka and Maharashtra. He suggests that the composition of the Chennakesava *mulaprasada* and its stellate form would not look out of place in central India, homeland of Nagara *Bhumija* temples. In addition, the predominance of Nagara superstructures on the miniature shrines indicate that the Chennakesava is indeed a Nagara temple, characterised entirely, however, by regional idiom. The Hoysala *Bhumija* superstructures, for instance, have hardly any curvature. They are conceived as "tightly-stepped pyramids", their squat proportions reflecting the local model [66]. Despite the success of the Chennakesava, however, Nagara temples were rare among Hoysala constructions. Only five Hoysala temples out of over a hundred studied by Foekema have Nagara aedicules[67.] Del Bonta suggests that the external wall articulation was not put into any future Hoysala styles because it was external in origin.[68] Since other northern features were copied this conclusion is rather questionable.

However, it is conceivable that, since the Chennakesava was a very early Hoysala temple, the new dynasty was still searching for a distinct "voice". Another early temple, the Lakshmidevi temple in Doddagadduvalli, has nine shrines, only one of which has an aedicular structure. The pyramidal superstructure of the other eight shrines amounts to a series of serrated horizontal *kapota*-like mouldings, decreasing in size, with deep recesses in between each one, described variously as Phamsana or a Phamsana hybrid, Kalinga or Kadamba. There is no suggestion here of the Dravida *shalas* and *kutas*, but the pyramidal shape and the stark horizontality strongly suggest

Dravida architecture, although Collyer disputes this, asserting that they resemble the Nagara style[69]

Fig 28. The Chennakesava Temple at Belur. Base mouldings

The *Kamikagama* refers to the Deccan as the Vesara area, thus including other, non-Hoysala temples. Kramrisch narrows it down to the Kanarese Later Chalukya areas and the Hoysala Mysore area[70]. Sinha concentrates on 11th century Later Chalukya temples in his work on Vesara, maintaining that these were an intentional modification of traditions through intervention based on local traditions. Although the first evidence of a break with Dravida tradition is seen in the 10th century temples at Aihole, Sinha argues that Vesara's origin was in the 11th century and was not an evolution from earlier temples as previously assumed[71]. Hardy maintains that it is impossible to say at what moment temples ceased to be Dravida and became Vesara[72] The greater complexity of plans in the form of staggered squares and projections facilitated the development of greater verticality and a suggestion of the curvilinear. The sandstone Yallama (Yellamagudi) temple in Badami and its plan can be seen in figs 29a and 29b. It is a Later Chalukya temple but there is no consensus on its construction date. Dhaky placing it in the 'formative phase of Vesara architecture', dates the Yallama to 1025 CE[73], Sinha refutes this, arguing that it is a 'mature and sophisticated example of Vesara architecture', and dates it to 1075-1100 CE[74]. Hardy suggests possibly 1139-40 CE[75]. It is a single *vimana* temple with five projections, four *talas* and double-staggered central *shala*-aedicules. Despite its completely Dravida articulation, its Vesara appearance is evident: the superstructure displays compressed horizontal storeys, and diminished articulation of architectural models. The central spine is accentuated due to the projecting *bhadra*. Large, decorated *nasis* enhance this still further.

Fig 29a. The Yallama (Yellamagudi) temple in Badami

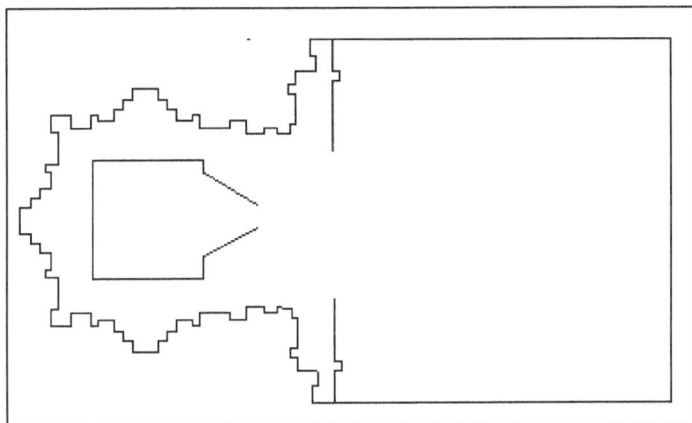

Fig 29b. Outline plan of the Yallama (Yellamagudi) temple in Badami

In short...

The temples known as Vesara or Karnata Dravida are a localised idiom in the Dravida language. Although they may bear a passing resemblance to some Nagara structures, their architecture, though not necessarily their ornamentation, is totally Dravida. Temples began to evolve in this manner during the Later Chalukya era or possibly earlier. The Hoysala contribution has been a greater complexity in the development of the plan, particularly the stellate forms, influencing the whole articulation of the temple, creating greater verticality and more room for ornamentation. Unparalleled dynamism is achieved through the stellate form, which gives a rotating, spinning, unfurling effect. The play of light and shade on the sharp angles of the walls increases the effect of rippling movement. The *vimanas* can be seen as the cosmos spinning through space and unfurling from the top downwards as they rotate. Cosmic forces can be seen as emerging from within different points. The stellate *vimana* is architecturally broken down into a large number of points and corners and components therefore fragmenting but at the same time the whole presents unification and fusion, thus paralleling the disintegration and reabsorbing of the cosmos. Despite some experimentation with non-Dravida temples, most of the Hoysala *vimanas* evolved from the Karnata Dravida or Vesara idiom. The next chapter will consider whether there is any relationship between the evolution of the *vimana* and the development of Hoysala temple sculpture.

Chapter 4: Not without beauty: Hoysala sculpture and ornamentation

The splendour of soapstone

A result of increasingly complex stellate or staggered-square *vimanas* was additional exterior surface area, which could be exploited sculpturally. This was facilitated by the use of chloritic schist, also known as potstone or soapstone, as the main construction material. Soapstone is soft when first exposed to air but gradually hardens over time. The compact molecules make the stone ideal for carving and polishing[76]. According to Harle the deep undercutting and carving that it enabled gave "the richest surface texture … in India…" [77]. There are several colours including green, blue-black, cream, gold and its texture is ideal for fine carving. Settar refers to it as "soft as a piece of chalk" [78], which may be somewhat overstated.

Of the twelve temples in this study, only one, the Panchalingeshwara temple in Somnathapur is not constructed of soapstone, but granite, the principal stone of the Somnathapur area. The pillars of the Govindanahalli Panchalingeshwara are also granite, but the temple building is of soapstone[79]. Fig 30 shows the distribution of some of the most important Karnata Dravida temples, with major sites labelled. The map shows the building materials used for major Hoysala and Later Chalukya temples, and confirms that the main Hoysala temples were predominantly built of soapstone, which can be found in the Halebid area.

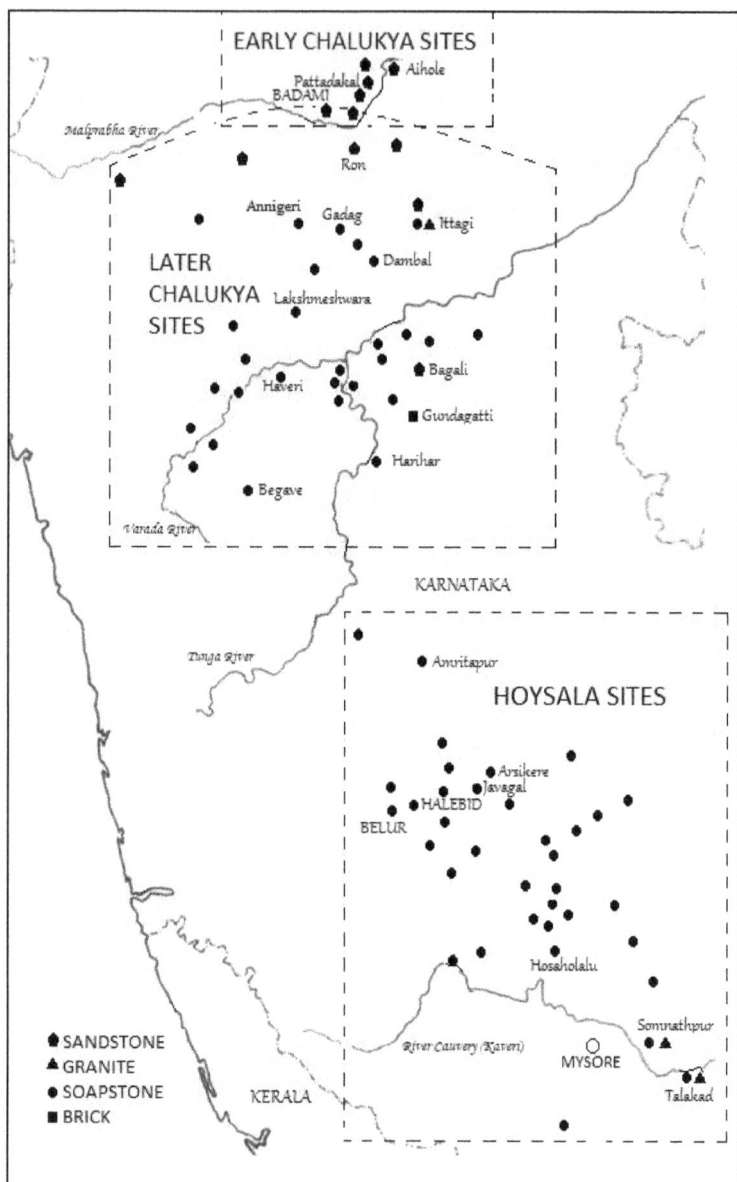

EARLY CHALUKYA SITES

Aihole
Pattadakal
BADAMI
Malprabha River

Ron

LATER
CHALUKYA Lakshmeshwara
SITES

Annigeri
Gadag
Dambal
Ittagi

Bagali
Haveri
Gundagatti

Harihar

Begave

Varada River

KARNATAKA

Tunga River

Amritapur

HOYSALA SITES

Arsikere
Javagal
HALEBID
BELUR

Hosaholalu

Somnathpur

River Cauvery (Kaveri)

MYSORE

Talakad

♠ SANDSTONE
▲ GRANITE
● SOAPSTONE
■ BRICK

KERALA

Fig 30. Distribution of Karnata Dravida temples, showing material used for construction.

58

However, a large number of Later Chalukya temples, much further north than the Hoysala ones, were also built in soapstone. Foekema suggests that soapstone was introduced by the Later Chalukyas after they took power from the Rastrakutas in 973 CE, and dates examples of its first use to the middle of the 11th century, one of the earliest defining soapstone temples being the Amriteshwara in Annigeri (Fig 31) [80]. Soapstone was to remain the main medium of building from the late 10th to the mid-14th century[81].

Fig 31. The Amriteshwara Temple in Annigeri: Later Chalukya second half of the 11th century CE

The map also shows that Later Chalukya temples along The Malaprabha River were invariably built in sandstone, the principal stone of the area, but that those in the rest of Karnataka were predominantly soapstone. The occasional appearance of granite temples among these and the Hoysala soapstone temples, suggests that possibly granite or other materials were used for less prestigious temples. Rangaraju suggests that granite temples were rare except in the Tamil Nadu areas of the Hoysala realm[82].

The only conclusions that can be drawn therefore are that most major Hoysala temples were built in soapstone, which was clearly regarded as valuable building material. This is illustrated by the Kesava temple in Somnathapur, which was prestigious enough for the soapstone to be imported into the area.

Ornateness: all frills and froth?

Hardy suggests that the use of soapstone was connected with a regional predilection for complexity and fine detail[83]. He refutes the arguments that the material determined the style of the temple, maintaining that the style was essentially formed before soapstone was introduced, as evidenced by instances of fine polished flesh and minutely cut jewel-like sculpture from non-soapstone temples of the Later Chalukya era, without, however, the "overladen aspect of much Hoysala sculpture"[84]. He classifies ornateness as one of the defining characteristics of Hoysala temples, pointing to the possibilities offered by soapstone. These are exemplified by a door lintel of the Hoysaleshwara in Halebid (fig 32), showing dancing forms of Shiva flanked by smaller Vishnu and Brahma images embedded in the deeply undercut, lacy *makara torana*.

Hardy refers to the ornateness of figure sculptures and the banded plinths, but also the "character of the carving and the degree of elaboration" on the mouldings and the "grooved, bored, drilled and undercut" soapstone[85].

Fig 32 Halebid, Hoysaleshwara, Halebid door lintel

Also typical of ornateness is the *kapota* (and also *chadya*) fringe, which, while occurring on the some Later Chalukya temples, was "taken a step further by the Hoysalas, with the introduction of the double fringe"[86]. Fig 33 shows the Kesava in Somnathapur, in which the double fringe and the imitation wood underside of the *chadyas* are clearly visible. The double fringe is made up of rows of pearly garlands, with rows of stone droplets seemingly "hanging" beneath.

Commonly found at the ends of schematic *shala* roof components (fig 23) of an ornate temple are "diagonal *nasis*" (fig 34). Although seen on some Later Chalukya temples they became "virtually universal" on Hoysala temples[87]. It is not possible to make a definitive assessment of these temples due to loss or restoration of superstructure on at least four of them. However, the ornate temples at Doddagadduvalli, Belvadi, Arsikere, Hosaholalu, Javagal, and Somanthpur all have prominent diagonal *nasis*.

Fig 33. Somnathapur, Kesava: the two chadyas, both double-fringed and also showing the wood imitation underside to the upper chadya.

Fig 34.
Belvadi,
Viranaryana:
diagonal nasis
on the closed
mandapa roof

However, ornateness should not be confused with form. Hardy warns against confusing ornamental elements with compositional ones. Simply because a temple is more ornate, does not mean that it is more complex[88.] This can be illustrated by comparing the *vimana* of the Lakshminarasimha temple at Javagal (fig 35) with the Anantapadmanabha temple at Hosabubnur (fig 36). Both temples have five projections on each side of the *vimana* and intermediate *kuta* aedicules. They are both Dravida structures, although the base mouldings of the Javagal temple have mutated into friezes. Both temples are divided by a central *chadya* and have a second *chadya* beneath the *kapota* at the top. Both temples have the compressed schematic Dravida superstructure that is associated with Karnata Dravida temples and both stand on a platform. A cursory glance might suggest that the Javagal temple is the more complex, since it is covered with ornate carvings. Foekema classifies the superstructure decoration at Javagal as the "most lavish to be found in Hoysala architecture"[89]. On the other hand, the Hosabudnur temple is unadorned. However, the temple at Javagal has three *talas*, whereas the Hosabudnur temple has four. Moreover while the Javagal temple has single-staggered central aedicules, the Hosabudnur temple has double-staggered central aedicules. So, far from being less complex than its ornate counterpart, the Hosabudnur temple is structurally the more complex.

Fig 35. Javagal, Lakshminarasimha: vimana

Fig 36. Hosabudnur, Ananthapadmanabha: vimana

Whereas Hardy distinguishes between abundance of figure sculpture and ornateness[90], Foekema draws a distinction between ornamental architectural components (ie those that contribute to the decoration of temple, not part of the temple structure) and figure sculpture. He concedes that the two are easily confused because architectural components may include some figures and figure sculpture may include some architectural components. He defines architectural components as "belonging to a pattern that gives shape to the whole shrine". Figure sculpture he defines as representations standing "on (sic) themselves"[91]. These are important distinctions when considering the uniqueness of Hoysala temples. Although a temple like the Later Chalukya Yellamagudi in Badami (fig 29b) is richly decorated in terms of architectural components it has little in the way of figural ornamentation except on the superstructure. This can be said of many Later Chalukya temples. However, architectural ornamentation also featured large in Hoysala temples, as can be seen on the Chennakesava temple at Marle (fig 89).

Wall images: the temple as a sculpture gallery

The more ornate tendencies were certainly given impetus by Vishnuvardhana's conversion to Srivaishnavism from Jainism. In particular what Del Bonta calls the polytheism of Srivaishnavism gave the opportunity for many representations of Vishnu and the creation of much imagery[92]. Del Bonta implies the combination of "vocabulary from a variety of sources" in a new way. He suggests a desire for new Indian dynasties to create a statement[93]. It is, above all, the abundance of figural sculpture that sets some Hoysala temples apart. Whereas some less decorated Hoysala temples could be mistaken for Later Chalukya ones, those with a profusion of large wall images are impossible to mistake for anything other than Hoysala temples. Settar maintains that Hoysala art is not gradual having been in place from the start of the 12th century

All the art (except in the Tamil areas and one or two exceptions in Belur) shares the same features. One cannot say that 12th century art is better than 13th century. There is no stylistic variation between Hoysala artists, whether they are signed or unsigned. The differences in the workmanship are "unmistakable but indefinable"[94].. Conformity was valued over individuality. Innovations were evolved by the architect. The sculptors' innovations were always made in moderation.

The first, and some would argue the finest, temple to manifest a multitude of wall images was the Chennakesava at Belur. The large soapstone wall images on the exterior of the *vimana* depict deities and their attendants, including numerous Shaiva images. While this is unusual in a Vaishnava temple, it is by no means unique. The wall carvings show deep undercutting, making figures stand out sharply against their shadows. One Chalukyan artist, Dasojana, has has left his signature on several figures, confirming that the Later Chalukya influence is still strong here. The Chennakesava is not over-endowed with imagery, and the exterior images do not display the crowded detail that can be seen on later temples. Fig 37 shows a wall image of Shiva destroying the elephant demon. It has no *torana*, the ornamentation is sparse and the surrounding wall is left bare. It is surmounted by a Nagara superstructure. On the Chennakesava the architectural form takes priority, notably the huge *stambha*-aedicules on the *vimana* (fig 38).

Images of deities, human, animal and mythical figures abound within the temple. The *dvarapalas* at Belur guarding the cult deity of Kesava are regarded stylistically as among the finest in Hoysala art. They stand in *tribhanga* pose either side of the doorway and their enormous height can be seen by the shrine *dvarapala* in fig 39. Polished to a black shine, they are flanked by the wall-pilasters from which spring intricately carved *toranas* [95].

Fig 37. *Belur,*
Chennakesava Temple
Shiva destroying the
elephant demon

Fig 38. Belur, Chennakesava Temple vimana

Fig 39. Chennakesava Temple, Belur: dvarapala

Outright eroticism was eschewed by the Hoysalas but they expressed female nudity in other ways, such as the *madanakai* (bracket figure) in fig 40, who is tussling with a monkey that is pulling off her sari. This is probably a reference to the

Mahabharata episode involving the attempted disrobing of Draupadi in the Kaurava Court. Draupadi was saved by the intervention of Krishna, who supplied her with an endless garment, thereby safeguarding her honour. Like Chennakesava, Krishna is, of course, a form of Vishnu.

Fig 40. Belur, Chennakesava: madanakai

Male nudity, like female, was avoided where possible[96]. The *madanakais*, female figures derived from the Buddhist *shalabhanjikas*, were already well known in the Later Chalukya Lakkundi School. The *madanakais* at Belur, however, are thought by many art historians to be unsurpassed. Of the original forty, thirty-eight are still in place. The extreme delicacy of the carving was probably possible because they have no architectural function[97]. They are also noted for their successful realisation of movement. Evidence indicates that the *madanakais* were not part of the original design but were attached later to the pillars. Smaller human figure brackets with rearing lions can be seen behind them, more obviously integral to the pillar. An inscription beneath a *madanakai* refers to Vishnuvardhana, and since inscriptions on the *madanakais* suggest that the artists came from north of the Hoysala District, Vishnuvardhana would have had enough power towards the end of his reign to employ them to carve the *madanakais*, possibly between 1133 and 1142 CE[98]. Settar describes this as tribal art, which displayed a childish pleasure in minute detail, variety and extravaganza. Controversially he suggests that only the *malepas* could fully appreciate it, which, whilst only an opinion, is a reminder of the role of the "period eye"[99].

The Hoysaleshwara temple in Halebid has approximately 594 external reliefs[100], probably more than anywhere else in India[101.] It has the largest wall images of all Hoysala temples. Almost every inch of the back half of the temple has been covered below the second *chadya*, including the recesses, some sculptures buried deep in the architecture, all merging into what amounts to a huge, horizontal frieze as can be seen in fig 62a. This is in stark contrast to Belur. Full advantage has been taken of the shadow and light play and the extra space created by the stellate and staggered form. The figures appear to have been carved almost in the round, and burst out of the wall. The large wall images are 1.5 metres high including *toranas*, foliage and pedestals. Many show smaller musicians playing to dancing deities, evidence of the importance of dance to the Hoysalas. Stances include exaggerated curves and overemphasised fluidity in order to convey dance movement. Vishnu is extensively depicted in all his forms on this Shaiva temple, particularly as Kesava, Narasimha, Varaha and various forms of Krishna. There are a few *madanakais* but most have disappeared. Those remaining are not placed diagonally but extend along the beams, suggesting that they were part of the original construction and not an "add on" as in Belur[102].

Although the proportions, decorative vocabulary and general composition of the sculptures are similar in Belur and Halebid variations and additions occur[103]. The artist was clearly searching for something different from his predecessors. As a result, Settar suggests that, compared with the *dvarapalas* guarding the Kesava icon in Belur, those guarding the *linga* in the Hoysaleshwara have been reduced to dummies on which to hang fantastic jewellery[104]. Fig 41 shows one of the Halebid *dvarapalas*, which is clearly more elaborately garlanded and bejewelled than its Belur counterpart (fig 39). It has also become squatter and its facial features less animated, pointing to a move towards minor adjustments of physical proportion and ornamental arrangements that became typical of Hoysala art, probably reflecting the features of the Hoysala tribe.

The carvings on the outer walls of the Panchalingeshwara temple at Govindanahalli are of the "smaller" variety[105]. Many are Vaishnava as in fig 42, including, on the eastern side, the *Vishnucaturvimsati*. There are several dancing figures including Thandareshwara, a dancing Ganesh and a dancing Saraswati in *tribangha* posture. Either side of the entrances are the *dvarapalas*, one of each pair signed by Mallitamma, whose signature is carved into the rock under the feet of the *dvarapalas* in fig 43. The mixed iconography of the Panchalingeshwara suggests that it may originally have been intended as a syncretic temple rather than the present arrangement of five *lingas* in a row[106].

Fig 41. Halebid,
Hoysaleshwara: dvarapala

Fig 42. Govindanahalli: Panchalingeshwara temple. Small wall
images (D Black)

Fig 43. Govindanahalli: Panchalingeshwara temple.: dvarapala

The Ishwara Temple at Arsikere has a horizontal "frieze" of some 120 "smaller" variety wall images running around the closed *mandapa,* the *sukhanasi* and the *vimana* (fig 44). Although Arsikere is a Shiva temple the outer walls of the *vimana* are dominated by Vishnu. These images have been executed with great delicacy. They include the twenty-four forms of Vishnu and six images depicting Shiva and Parvati. The deities are mainly standing, and only differ in the attributes they carry. The Shaiva images are on the *navaranga* walls. There is a marked absence of dancing deities and attendant figures in the sculptures, instead an emphasis on still, elegant poses. The mixed iconography of this temple was arguably an important step in the development of joint temples in the form of Harihara[107].

Fig 44. Arsikere, Ishwara: wall images

Girdling the *vimanas* and the closed hall of the Lakshminarayana temple in Hosaholalu are sixty-one wall images. These include some Shaiva images. Fig 45 shows a dancing Parvati with Ganesh and Murugan. There are, however, no direct images of Shiva. Also depicted are most of the forms of Vishnu. Fig 46 shows Krishna dancing on the subdued serpent Kaliya. The images are about 1.2 metres high including their *torana* and pedestals. Mallitamma may have been the sculptor here, due to apparent similarity to sculptures at the Lakshminarasimha temple at Nuggihalli[108]. There does not, however, seem to be any documentary evidence to support this. Indeed Foekema suggests that the decoration, although detailed, is repetitive, sometimes on the "threshold of art but never with the pretensions of it"[109].

Fig 45.
Lakshminarayana
temple in
Hosaholalu:
dancing Parvati
with Ganesh and
Murugan (D
Black)

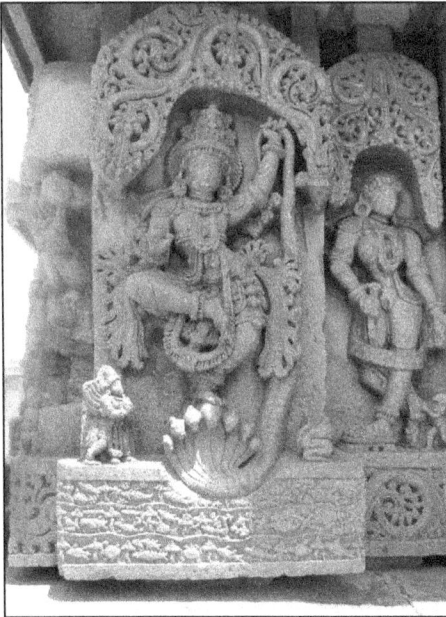

Fig 46.
Lakshminarayana
temple in
Hosaholalu:
Krishna subduing
the serpent Kaliya
(D Black)

Seventeen of the 141 large wall images of the Lakshminarasimha temple at Javagal are signed by Mallitamma. Mallitamma's working life appears to have been from 1196 to 1268, which implies that there was more than one sculptor of that name[110]. Collyer suggests that possibly the name was, in the later stages at least, attributed to his workshop but that the Javagal sculptures are early works resembling the *dvarapalas* at Govindanahalli, and implying an early date in Mallitamma's career for both temples. She regards some of the Javagal images, as stiff and upright, as befits a god. She refers to the increasing stockiness of occasional wall images at Javagal that will become the predominant style of later Hoysala images[111]. Foekema, however, sees some of the sculpture at Javagal as more relaxed than other Hoysala sculpture[112].

As is usual in a Vaishnava temple, the large wall images are nearly all of Vishnu. One obvious exception is the dancing Ganesh, the god that appears on most temples (fig 48). This carving is very animated as can be seen from comparing it with the same deity at Hosaholalu (fig 47). While the one at Hosaholalu has more lavish surroundings, the elaborate, heavy floral bower, and the poses are similar, the one at Javagal is the livelier and less rigid figure. The Javagal figure is signed by Chikka Mallitamma, who is assumed to be Mallitamma's son.

The walls of the Kesava temple in Somnathapur are home to 194 large images. They are more or less at the viewer's eye level, due partly to lower placing than in some earlier temples and partly to the compact nature of the Kesava. Most of the images, placed on each side of the regular star points, are a form of Vishnu. Many are now unidentifiable. Some are Vishnu's *avatars*, others are Vaishnava myths or local forms. Other variations include postures and hand *mudras*. Yet others are concerned with the attributes that the god is holding in one of his several hands such as the *gada*, the *chakra*, the *shanka* and the *padma*. There are countless variations including *mudras* displayed by the additional arms. Other deities, such as Saraswati and Lakshmi dance on the walls.

Fig 47. Lakshminarayana temple,
Hosaholalu: dancing Ganesh

Fig 48. Lakshminarasimha temple,
Javagal: dancing Ganesh

The large images on the southern *vimana* are particularly lively. Among them is a dancing Ganesh on the first panel (fig 49a). Ganesh as usual is placed at the beginning to ensure future success. However, in this instance there is another dimension. The *Ramayana* frieze directly underneath this image of Ganesh depicts the birth of the four brothers Rama, Lakshmana, Bharata and Satrughna, the heroes of the epic (fig 49b). It is no accident that Ganesh, the god of good fortune, was placed directly above this panel. The large wall images are not always relevant to the epic panel beneath them, but a relationship can often be identified[113].

Fig 49a. Somnathapur, Kesava: dancing Ganesh above the Ramayana frieze showing the birth of the four brothers.

Here also, many sculptures are signed. This departure from the usual anonymity of Indian sculptors gives some insight into the probable social ethos during the Hoysala era, in this case the reign of Narasimha III. It suggests a time of considerable freedom, the expression of free will and pride in artistic achievements. Thirty large sculptures are definitely the work of Mallitamma but over eighty bear a name that may also be a variation of Mallitamma. Some less accomplished sculptures attributed to him may have been the work of an apprentice. Comparing this work with his earlier work, the zigzag wall surface gives a more even light distribution and may be the reason that Mallitamma and other sculptors cut more deeply than in earlier temples. The conventional style may have been imposed by the workshop and also relates the static poses and the verticality of the sculptures to the increasing verticality of the whole temple imposed by the star-shaped plan[114].

Fig 49b. Kesava Temple, Somnathapur: The birth of the 4 brothers. Ramayana frieze, southern vimana.

The Chalukyan influence on the Hoysala sculptural style is undeniable. However, while it is possible to mistake Hoysala sculpture for Later Chalukya sculpture, it is arguably impossible to mistake it for any other school since Hoysala ornaments differ in workmanship from Early Chalukyan, Pallava and Chola ornamentation[115]. Settar refers to the long, conical crown, narrow face and pointed chin of the Mohini at the Chennakesava in Belur (fig 50) as combining Chola and Chalukyan features. He indicates an innovative downward expansion of the belly immediately below the breasts in female Hoysala figures and also a much lower expansion of the pelvic section. There is increased surface modulation such as horizontal belly mouldings. Male figures are shorter, and less

79

flat or smooth than other schools. They show a lack of balance between the torso and the "powerful arms" and stumpy legs, making the figures appear lifeless[116]. He comments on the rigidity of even moving, dancing or flexed sculptures of humans and deities in human form such as the Mahishasuramardini on the wall of the Hoysaleshwara (fig 51). Deities depicted in animal form are more "successful", as fig 52 shows[117]. Evans[118] sees Hoysala goddesses as beautiful even in their terrifying forms. Harle found Hoysala images, although "not without beauty", also particularly suited to the *ugra* form[119.]

Fig 50 Belur, Chennakesava temple: Mohini Pillar

Fig 51. Halebid, Hoysaleshwara temple: Mahishasuramardini.

Fig 52. Halebid, Hoysaleshwara temple: Dancing Ganesh.

Hoysala art can be seen against the tribal background of the founders. Settar believes the artists stuck to the "conceptualised ideals" of the *Silpa* texts (the rules relating to proportion, shapes and forms of an adolescent body). However, the details were left to the artists. He proposes an interesting theory that the human form of Hoysala sculptures resembles that of their tribe: plump and stumpy, like Malenadu tribals[120]. Collyer suggests only the sanctum images had to conform to traditional measurements, which were therefore generally taller and more elegant. Comparison of the icon of Janardhana in the northern shrine of the Kesava temple at Somnathapur (fig 53) with an exterior wall image (fig 54) supports this theory[121].

Somnathapur, Kesava temple

Fig 53. Janardhana icon

Fig 54. Vaishnava image exterior wall

Although there is no dispute about the unprecedented abundance of Hoysala figural sculpture, distinction in style is not always so easy to ascertain. Some Later Chalukya temples, particularly in the Kalyani region, are also extensively girdled by large wall images, though not yet amounting to the frieze-like quality of some of the Hoysala temples. One theory is that the Hoysala large wall image is derived from temples such as this, but even at an early stage the Hoysala images are more elaborately detailed[122].

To some extent, therefore, the supple, elegant early figural sculpture of Belur later gave way to forms that have been described as dwarfish, grotesque or squat. Ornamentation in the way of jewellery, clothing and background has been criticised as being distracting and over-elaborate. However, there is no disputing its jewel-like quality, which is perhaps owed to craftsmen around Mysore, used to working with sandalwood or ivory. It has also been suggested that there was little evolution in style throughout the Hoysala era, making it easy to confuse early and later works. Ample evidence of the Hoysala's love of dance is reflected in Hoysala temples. Many of the carved female figures depict postures associated with *Bharatanatyam*. Dancing deities and musicians are prominent. Whatever the individual merit of a particular carving the overall effect produced by a frieze of large wall images is unique to the Hoysalas.

The banded friezes: stories in stone

A major innovation in sculptural expression was the highly carved band of six or eight horizontal friezes, which run around the base of some Hoysala temples. The flat soapstone surfaces enabled prolific and detailed carving. These friezes, which are always staggered in keeping with the aedicular structure of the wall, can either be read as a vertical section belonging to the aedicule, or a horizontal section taking the place of the plinth[123].

Although the Chennakesava temple in Belur is the first example of the Hoysala ornate style, the absence of the banded friezes shows it is clearly still in its early stages of development. There are, in fact, eight basement friezes to the *navaranga* (fig 55), but these are not in the uninterrupted horizontal bands of later temples[124]. Hardy has argued that friezes appearing on the wall-shrines of the Chennakesava could be a prototype of the banded friezes (fig 56)[125]. However, evidence suggests that they could also be a later addition. This will be considered further in the next chapter.

Fig 55. Belur, Chennakesava: navaranga basement friezes

Fig 56. Belur,
Chennakesava:
Friezes on a wall shrine

The banded friezes may conceivably be related to northern and western practices[126]. According to Foekema, however, they had no predecessors and are consequently unique to the Hoysalas[127]. They did not evolve, but appeared as a fully formed, new feature in around 1125 CE in the eight friezes of the Hoysaleshwara in Halebid, breaking over five centuries of Karnata Dravida tradition regarding the articulation of the plinth. However, despite their innovativeness, they are not a complete rupture with the past. As already shown in figs 24b & c, remnants of mouldings can still be made out in parts of the friezes on the Hoysaleshwara. The underside of the top one - the *hamsas* - has the shape of the *vedi (vedika)*; the next one - the *makaras,* has the wooden floor with joists structure of a metamorphosised *vyalamala*: note in particular the diagonal *makara* heads. The upper side of the third one (epic frieze) is shaped like the *kapota* [128]. These reminders do not appear in later temples such as the Kesava in Somnathapur. Bearing in mind this evolution from Dravida mouldings, it could be argued that any attempt to link the banded friezes to the Chennakesava in Belur is inappropriate, since, as has already been discussed, the Chennakesava is a Nagara structure.

Fig 57. Halebid, Hoysaleshwara: frieze band

The friezes on the Hoysaleshwara (fig 57) depict *hamsas*, *makaras*, epic narratives, vine scrolls reminding us of the affiliation between the temple and water symbolism, horses with riders, vine scrolls and leonine creatures. The temple is "supported" by the lowest frieze of some two thousand miniature elephants, no two of which appear to be alike. Many of the panels are carved so deeply that they appear to be almost in the round. Most of the bands are nine inches wide but the vine scrolls are narrower. In subsequent ornate temples the lions are frequently missing[129]. Many artists' signatures appear on the friezes. The epic band depicts the *Ramayana*, the *Mahabharata* and the *Bhagavata Puranas*. Mainly the narratives run in a clockwise direction, but occasionally an episode is the other way round. The *Bhagavata Purana* is on the east side of the *navaranga*. The *Mahabharata* and *Ramayana* scenes are somewhat haphazardly dotted around. The *Ramayana* in particular is very fragmented. The *Mahabharata* is considered the more accomplished work[130].

Fig 58. Hosaholalu, Lakshminarayana: a projecting stone in the elephant frieze bearing a carving of a yaksha inside a torana (D. Black)

The lowest frieze of the Lakshminarayana in Hosaholalu also depicts elephants. Unusually, the elephant frieze is interrupted in each aedicule by a projecting stone bearing a carving of a *yaksha* inside a *torana*, replicating the carving on the *harantara* and *panjara* roofs (fig 58).

The next frieze shows horse riders. Then comes a floral scroll. The epic frieze depicts the *Mahabharata*, the *Ramayana*, the *Bhagavata* and some isolated scenes from the *Puranas*. The top two friezes show elaborately decorated *makaras* and finally a row of *hamsas*. The six friezes encompass the whole temple, including the parapet wall.

The Lakshminarasimha temple at Javagal also has a band of six friezes running around it, apart from the porch area where only the lower four friezes are present. This gives weight to Foekema's theory that these four friezes form the pedestal and that the two upper friezes, the *hamsa* and *makara* friezes form the "lower end of the temple itself"[131]. The four lower friezes follow the usual pattern: elephants supporting the base, horse riders, a scroll frieze and an epic frieze. As always the friezes follow the contours of the plan. The *Mahabharata* is not thought to be depicted only the *Ramayana* and some mythological scenes[132]. However, fig 59 shows a scene that strongly resembles the dice game between the Pandavas and the Kauravas, casting doubt one this conclusion.

Fig 59. Javagal, Lakshminarasimha: dice game

The horizontality of the wall friezes of the Kesava temple at Somnathapur contrasts sharply with the verticality of the *vimana* superstructures, increasing the feeling of a changing and yet completely integrated scenario: in addition the architecture of the friezes follows the vertical contours of the aedicules.(Fig 60).

Fig 60. Somnathapur: western vimana

Fig 61 Somnathapur. Friezes at the Kesava Temple,

Only the lower four of the six base friezes are present on the open part of the *mandapa* (*navaranga*). The lowest frieze around the whole temple consists of 577 finely carved elephants. The stablising effect is combined with that of movement since the elephants appear to be marching briskly around the temple in a disciplined display of war and peace. The Hoysalas' intimate knowledge of these animals that are native to the area is clear. The next band shows a frieze of horsemen, equally lively as they control their rearing and galloping horses in battle. Above these are scrolls of creepers. The next frieze shows scenes from the *Ramayana* starting with the *durbar* of Dasaratha on the first panel and continuing along the southern *vimana*. At the *sukhanasi* of the southern *vimana* the four friezes become six with the addition of bands of *makaras* and *hamsas (Fig 61)*. The epic frieze around the central (western) *vimana* shows scenes from Krishna's life. The friezes on the northern *vimana* follow the same pattern as the others but now the epic frieze shows scenes from the *Mahabharata*. At the open part of the *mandapa* the pattern of four friezes is resumed. As in Halebid, many of the friezes are signed by the artist, in this case predominantly by Mallitamma.

While scenes from the epics had long been depicted on Indian temples, for instance on the pillars of the Virupaksha temple in Pattadakal, they had never before been seen in a continuous frieze. Their didactic purpose, placed at comfortable viewing level for devotees walking around the temple is clear. The platform, which will be discussed in the next chapter, encouraged close-up viewing of tiny, exquisitely detailed reliefs. The relationship between some of the scenes on the friezes and the large wall image immediately above emphasises the meaning of the story being told. While there seems to be a standard way of depicting episodes, differences again suggest a degree of artistic freedom, incorporating individual treatment of foliage and other decoration. This can be seen in figs 62a-g, which include two from the Kedareshwara temple in Halebid, not included in my twelve temples due to dubious restauration. The individual panels however, are of high quality. Fig 62c shows a great deal of originality in the depiction of the *Jatayusamhara* scene. Although the banded friezes came into existence on the Hoysaleshwara temple during the early and middle part of the 12th century, they were then abandoned until the 13th century. Only four of the twelve temples in this study have them.

Of some fifty-three Hoysala temples featured by Hardy in his 1995 study, only twelve are listed as having a banded plinth. This put into perspective what has come to be known as "the Hoysala style".

Fig 62a-d. Comparisons of frieze panels on different temples

a. *Hunting the golden deer, (Ramayana): Kesava, Somnathapur.*

b. *Hunting the golden deer, (Ramayana): Lakshminarasimha Javagal*

c. *The death of Bishma, (Mahabharata): Lakshminarayana,*
Hosaholalu

d. *The death of Bishma, (Mahabharata): Kedareshwara Halebid.*

e. Kedareshwara temple, Halebid.

f. Lakshminarayana, Hosaholalu.

g. Kesava temple, Somnathapur

The indispensible chadya

Architectural ornamentation was exemplified by the addition of a *chadya*, a large projecting eaves added between the body of the temple and the *kapota* of the superstructure, thus forming a double eaves. Its prominent size and overhang accentuates the horizontality of the first *tala*. The double-eaves *chadya* first made its appearance in Later Chalukya temples described by Hardy as non-mainstream[133]. Normally these *chadyas* were double-curved, smooth and undecorated. The *mandapa* and porch *chadyas* were generally larger than those on the *vimana*, and often had wood imitation rafters and lotus flower bosses beneath. An example is the Someshwara temple at Lakshmeshwar (fig 63a and b). A prototype may have been the porch eaves of the Early Chalukya Virupaksha temple in Pattadakal (fig 64). Hardy describes this as more of a *chadya* that a *kapota*.[134]

Fig 63a. Someshwara temple at Lakshneshwar: porch

Fig 63b. Someshwara temple at Lakshneshwar: porch rafters

[135]Fig 64. Pattadakal, Virupaksha: porch showing the chadya-like eaves. (Langeveld)

Every one of the Hoysala temples in this study has a *chadya* between the body and the superstructure. Study of the temples depicted by Foekema suggests that there are no or few Hoysala temples without this *chadya*. Here also the artists exploited the possibilities of soapstone by adding garlands and beaded edges[136].

It is, however, the addition of a second *chadya* dividing the first *tala* that is seen as a defining Hoysala feature[137]. This gives the appearance of two bodies, the lower one having figure sculpture and the upper one with decorative towers on pilasters. However, usually the pilasters appear to continue down behind the second *chadya*, for this *chadya* does not influence of the structure of the aedicules, but adds further horizontality just as the friezes do.

Although the second *chadya* has been defined by Foekema as "belonging" to New Dravida temples (described in the historiography review of this study)[138], some temples that do not have other New Dravida features also have a second *chadya*, blurring of the divide between Foekema's Old and New Dravida temple types. Hoysala temples can be seen as those with only an upper *chadya*, those with both *chadyas* but no wall images, and those with both *chadyas* and wall images.

Temples with only an upper *chadya* include:

1. The Chennakesava temple at Belur. There is no second *chadya*, but the wall-shrines display a second *chadya*, as shown in fig 86. As previously mentioned, there is a debate about whether these shrines were subsequently added to the temple.
2. The original (western) Viranarayana *vimana* of the Viranarayana temple at Belvadi (fig 65)
3. The Panchalingeshwara Temple at Govindanahalli (fig 13a).

4. The Ishwara temple at Arsikere. Fig 12b clearly shows the upper *chadya* beneath the *kapota* on the *vimana* and closed hall and the particularly large *chadya* on the open hall.

5. The Lakshmidevi temple at Doddagadduvalli. Although the Phamsana shrines have schematic superstructure they have a large *chadya* separating the body from this and the *chadya* on the Dravida Lakshmidevi shrine is very pronounced (fig 66).

Fig 65. Viranarayana temple at Belvadi: The original (western) Viranaryana vimana

Fig 66. Doddagadduvalli, Lakshmidevi shrine showing the heavy chadya. The chadya on a Phamsana roof can be seen behind it.

Temples with both the upper and lower *chadya* but no wall images include:

1. The Anantapadmanabha temple at Hosabudnur (fig 16a). As well as the upper deep *chadya*, a dividing *chadya* runs along the body section of the temple. Below the upper *chadya* the temple wall is decorated with pilasters, which continue down "behind" the lower *chadya*.

2. The Panchalingeshwara temple at Somnathapur (see fig 17a). There is a second *chadya* dividing the wall area. The walls are flat and pilastered, but unlike the flat walls at

Doddagadduvalli, these have a Dravida, not a Phamsana superstructure. Foekema regards the *vimanas* as a "strange mixture of simple and articulated elements"[139.]

Temples with both the upper and lower *chadya* and wall images include:

1. The Hoysaleshwara temple in Halebid. The upper *chadya* of the wall-shrines coincides with the lower *chadya* of the main temple body. The lower *chadya* of the wall-shrines separates two niches. At this early stage the pilasters do not yet run down behind the second *chadya* of the temple. This can be seen clearly on fig 67. The *chadyas* have imitation wooden struts beneath them and are festooned with strings of beads (fig 68).

2. The Lakshminarayana temple at Hosaholalu (fig 14b). The coinciding of the upper *chadya* of the wall-shrines with the lower *chadya* of the temple body also occurs here. The lower *chadya* of the wall-shrines also separates two niches. Here also, the pillars "run down" behind the second *chadya*.

3. The "new" parts of the Viranarayana temple at Belvadi. The northern and southern *vimanas* display a second *chadya* (figs 28a & b). The *chadya* on the open hall of this temple is particularly large (fig 11b). Unlike the other temples discussed in this category, the two *vimanas* do not have banded friezes, and as such could be said to constitute a fourth category of temples with *chadyas*.

4. The Lakshminarasimha temple in Javagal (Fig 15b). A heavy second *chadya* has pilasters "continuing" behind it.

5. The Kesava temple at Somnathapur (fig 60). This has perhaps the finest upper *chadya* of all running around the whole length of the temple, possibly constructed on this large scale to protect the wall images from rain, as is seen by its pronounced slope, rather than simply to enhance the beauty of the temple[140]. Another, smaller *chadya* runs along the walls of the northern and southern *vimanas* approximately two thirds of the way up from the base. The western *vimana* is slightly

different in that a separate *chadya* is incorporated in each of the miniature towers over the large wall images, and does not give the appearance of continuity as in the other two *vimanas*.

Fig 67. Halebid Hoysaleshwara: *showing chadyas and a wall shrine.*

Fig 68. Halebid Hoysaleshwara: *"rafters" and beading on chadya*

The heavy upper *chadya*, whilst found on some Later Chalukyas temples, is an ornamental architectural feature found on practically all Hoysalas temples. The prototype may have its origins in Early Chalukya works at Pattadakal. It is not, therefore, unique to Hoysala temples but its consistent appearance makes it a distinctive Hoysala hallmark. The second *chadya* was almost certainly a new feature introduced by the Hoysalas. Foekema terms it a defining feature, along with the banded friezes, of New Dravida. However, there are some Hoysala temples with a second *chadya* that do not have banded friezes, or indeed large wall images.

Lathe-turned pillars?

Intricate, ornate carvings were found in all the soapstone temples, including doorways, ceilings and the icon in the *garbhagriha*. The pillars in both later Chalukya and Hoysala temples have been subject to intense controversy. They are normally set on a square base but the body of the pillar is cylindrical, sometimes bell shaped and invariably resembling in part piles of perfectly circular, sharp-edged plates of varying sizes and thickness. They are frequently richly carved or stellate. Some examples can be seen in figs 69a-d. Fig 69d serves as a reminder that some of the finest Hoysala work is found in Jain temples.

The belief that that the pillars could not have been formed by the unaided hand of man and must have been created by some sort of lathe was originally a theory suggested by Meadows Taylor writing in 1866, who noted, "it is impossible to … estimate how they were completed…without they were turned in a lathe"[141.] This theory was then taken up by other scholars and gradually accepted as fact. Percy Brown stated, "the pillars themselves took on a special form owing to a mechanical process by which they began to be produced..."[142]

Fig 69. "Lathe-turned" pillars in Hoysala temples

a. Kikkeri, Brahmeswara

b. Marle, Siddeshwara

c. Belur, Chennakesava

d. Halebid, Jain temple

However, no contemporaneous documentary evidence of lathe-turning has been found. This has led Settar to question the assumption that mechanical help was employed, arguing that if other fine carvings could be produced "freehand", it is perfectly feasible that craftsmen were able to create the pillars, concluding that if "what he produced with his hands was mistaken for a mechanical production", this "bears testimony to the excellent workmanship mastered by the Chalukya-Hoysala artist"[143]. Settar's assertion, however, assumes the same kind of skill required to achieve ornate figural carving as to create perfect geometrical circles and cylindrical shapes from massive stone blocks.

A more probable, but equally remarkable explanation is that the circular shapes were created on a lathe, and that the additional embellishments and star-cut edges were added by hand. It is possible that the lathe was turned with the aid of water[144]. Another suggestion is that animals, possibly elephants, drove the lathes[145]

The introduction of soapstone facilitated greater precision. Round pillars with circular plate-like layers are also found in Later Chalukya temples. Figs 70 and 71 show the pillars of the *mandapa* of the early 12th century Later Chalukya Sambhulinga temple at Kundgol and those at Belvadi. Pillars in both temples display precision work of a high standard. However, all the soapstone pillars inside Hoysala temples display fine detail, sharpness, highly polished reflective surfaces and mathematical perfection, whereas more research on the interior of Later Chalukya temples is needed. Hardy refrains from discussing Hoysala pillars in detail, suggesting that they are "very close to the non-mainstream of Northern Karnataka"[146]. However, they are of such extraordinary quality that they must be regarded as a distinctive, if not unique feature of Hoysala architecture.

Fig 70. Kundgol: mandapa of the Later Chalukya Sambhulinga temple

Fig 71. Belvadi: Viranaryana temple mandapa

105

In short...

The extra space created by increasing the complexity of temple form and plan coupled with the versatility of soapstone enabled the Mysore artisans, skilled in carving ivory and sandalwood, to push out the boundaries of sculptural possibility by developing and embellishing features already seen in earlier temples. These include the upper *chadya*, diagonal *shala*-end *nasis*, "lathe-turned" pillars, exterior wall images and ornate carvings. It has been seen that figure sculpture created by Hoysala artists developed different characteristics from that of the Later Chalukyas. Human forms tended towards squat rigidity, even in dancing poses, were generally festooned in lace-like clothing and jewellery, and surrounded by crowded figures, foliage and *toranas*. The Hoysalas also introduced entirely new sculptural features, both architectural and figural in the form of a second *chadya* and a band of friezes around the base of the temple. The next chapter will consider whether these developments are reflected in the layout of the temple.

Chapter 5: Public and private passions: The layout and surroundings

In previous chapters we saw that within the Hoysala realms the imposition of increasingly complex stellate and staggered square plans on to the Dravida aedicule resulted in a distinct *vimana* structure. The use of chloritic schist coupled with the extra surfaces created by this increased complexity facilitated innovative and abundant sculpture, which in the hands of artists skilled in the detailed carving of wood and ivory, was unprecedented and distinct. Were these developments related to developments in the layout and surroundings of the temple? It is clear from the emphasis on external sculpture that the Hoysala architects and artists considered the exterior of the temple of great importance. The sculpture on Hoysala temples is extremely detailed, and often miniaturised. The subject matter of the carving may also be relevant. The epic friezes, for example, are created in narrative form, like a comic strip that must be read from beginning to end. The prevalence of dancing deities and musicians suggests the importance of dance. Are these features related to the layout of the temple?

From the twelve temples in this study it appears that there is no such thing as a "typical" Hoysala layout. However, some features arise too frequently to be considered random. Chief among these are the raised platform which features in six of the twelve temples, the giant wall-shrines seen at six temples, the combined closed and open hall found at nine of the temples and the *prakara* wall, evidence for which was found at five temples.

Sacred mountain: the raised platform

Hardy suggests that the raised platform, unknown in other areas of South India, reflects the northern *jagati*[147]. The platforms of northern temples were broad and rectangular and often ornamented with mouldings[148]. This can be seen in fig 72 showing the Devi Jagadamba temple at Khajuraho dating from the late 11th century.

Fig 72. Devi Jagadamba temple, Khajuraho

However, the Hoysala platform, unlike the northern *jagati*, reflects the shape of the temple itself. Only one Later Chalukya temple stands on a platform, the Mallikarjuna at Sudi, which is relatively distant from Hoysala style, since it was built around 1050, and constructed of sandstone.[149] It is raised on a platform that is much wider than those of the Hoysala temples and only very roughly follows the temple contours, suggesting possibly influence from northern temples such as the above-mentioned one at Khajuraho. Even if the Hoysalas were influenced by the Mallikarjuna platform they expanded the idea, creating a unique regional version. It is, of course, entirely possible that the northern, Chalukyan and Hoysala platforms are completely unrelated, having sprung up independently.

The Kesava temple in Somnathapur (fig 18b) stands on a metre high platform, whose sixteen-point stellate form around the three *vimanas* compliments the form of the temple. Steps lead up onto the platform and into the temple in its eastern wall. Miniature shrines stand on either side of the steps. The platform has a markedly horizontal aspect due to the very deep mouldings. It is about three metres wide, allowing ample room for *pradakshina*. The platform is flanked by elephants around a metre high carved in the round standing against the angles of the platform as symbolic supports.

The Chennakesava temple at Belur stands on a moulded three-metre wide platform that also reflects the star shape of the temple. The steps leading onto the platform are flanked by miniature shrines (fig 73). Hardy (maintains that the platform moulding sequence of *vedi pitha jagati* reflects the simplified sequence of Nagara temple mouldings and that the same pattern is reflected in the pedestal of consecrated images[150]. He suggests a possible conscious analogy between the pedestal and raised platform[151].

The raised platform of the double complex of the Hoysaleshwara temple in Halebid also follows its contours. It has a mouldings sequence similar to that of the Chennakesava[152]. Four flights of steps lead up the platform to four flights of entrance steps, also flanked by miniature shrines (fig 74).

Fig 73. Belur, Chennakesava showing the star-shaped platform, the steps leading up from the paved courtyard and the miniature Nagara shrines

Fig 74. Halebid, Hoysaleshwara: steps to platform flanked by miniature shrines.

Rangaraju maintains that the Anantapadmanabha temple in Hosabudnur has no *jagati* but is built on "an eminence made of stone pieces and earth"[153]. He uses the northern term *jagati* to refer to the platform. Foekema, however, who, like Rangaraju, also saw the temple in its collapsed state, mentions that it has a platform[154]. Hardy also refers to it as a temple on a platform[155.] Certainly in its restored state it has a platform, following the contours of the temple. The Lakshminarasimha temple at Hosaholalu (fig 14b) stands on a raised platform approximately 1.4 metres high that follows the contours of the temple. Like the Kesava in Somnathapur, large stone elephants guard its cardinal points Settar suggests that elephants in the round symbolically support only a few temple platforms. Miniature shrines, such as those flanking the steps at Halebid and Belur, are more usual. Freestanding guardian elephants are not always associated with platforms. For example, the Chennakesava temple at Marle and the Viranarayana temple at Belvadi have them at entrances but do not have platforms. *Gajas* (elephants) as symbolic guardians of the *dik* (direction) are an ancient tradition in Karnataka, even found at Early Chalukya sites in Aihole and Pattadakal. They are found among Rastrakuta temples but less on Later Chalukya ones[156]. The Hoysalas repopularised the elephants and the miniature shrines.

The platform's function as a *pradakshinapatha* is fundamental, since no Hoysala temples have an internal *pradakshinapatha*. It is possible that the *pradakshina* around Hoysala temples had a didactic as well as symbolic purpose. This is particularly clear in the case of the narrative sculptures. The epic friezes are very small, the height of each frieze measuring around nine inches, therefore they have to be seen close-up. Only by circumambulation could the epic stories be "read". Rangaraju contrasts this with Chola sculptures, which have to be viewed from a distance[157]. Of the six temples with platforms in this study, only the Anantapadmanabha temple at Hosabudnur does not have epic friezes. Of the Hoysala temples listed by Hardy, only two of twelve with frieze-bands (both in Nagalpura) do not stand on a platform[158]. Hardy suggests that this is because the platform is submerged[159]. These results indicate a relationship between the presence of narrative friezes and a platform.

However, it could be argued that a ground level pavement around the temple would be just as effective for viewing, though perhaps not as focusing as a platform. Were the frieze-bands therefore the main reason for the platform? Of forty-one temples without frieze-bands listed by Hardy at least nine stand on a platform. This suggests that there may have been other important factors. The raised platform increases the movement upwards towards the mountain abode of the gods. It also serves to demarcate the sacred from the secular. Structurally the temples are quite low, possibly due to the weight-bearing limitations of soapstone. When soft, soapstone was unable to take the weight of the temple structure and hence the walls were often built of a middle section of earth and rubble encased between granite and the outer wall finally dressed with large blocks of soapstone that also helped to take the weight as they hardened[160]. Rangaraju suggests that architects maintained a uniform temple size because large soapstone pillars, unlike the granite pillars of Chola temples would not withstand the weight of heavy superstructure[161]. Crucially then, the platform adds height to the temple. This factor may have been of overriding concern to the Hoysala patrons when constructing their more important temples, whether plain or ornate.

Grand entrances: Compound walls and gateways

The desire to create an illusion of increased volume and grandeur may also explain the presence of a *prakara* wall around a number of temples. This subject is anything but straightforward. It is acknowledged in an oblique way by Hardy, who circumvents any definitive statement regarding the distinctiveness of the *prakara* wall to Hoysala architecture. He merely states that several Hoysala temples "retain their original compound walls", while Later Chalukya temples are "now" situated in open areas or hemmed in by houses[162]. However, the *prakara* wall with its gateway was a South Indian feature from late Early Chalukya times in temples such as the Virupaksha in Pattadakal.

Therefore two possibilities present themselves: either the wall fell out of favour during the Later Chalukya era or the Later Chalukya compound walls have all been lost. The latter seems unlikely considering the existing earlier examples at Pattadakal and the later or concurrent Hoysala examples. This suggests that the Hoysalas looked back to an earlier era and reinvented the *prakara* as a distinct Hoysala feature.

At least five of the twelve temples in this study are surrounded by a wall. However, it is not always easy to determine whether this wall is original. In addition, at least two other temples retain gateways and other features that suggest the former presence of a wall. By far the best known *prakara* wall surrounds the courtyard of the Kesava temple at Somnathapur. It has approximately fifty cellas with double or quadruple ones in the corners. A corridor runs around it in front of the cellas. "Lathe-turned" pillars produce a cloistered effect as shown in fig 75a. This wall enhances the unity and harmony of the entire Kesava complex. The icons in the cellas have long disappeared. A gateway (*mahadvara or dvaramandapa*) on the eastern side has "lathe-turned" pillars and resembles an open *mandapa*. Steps lead down into the courtyard (figs 75b and c).

The Lakshmidevi temple at Doddagadduvalli, some 150 years older than the Kesava, is surrounded by a plain wall without inset cellas but with attached corner shrines (fig 7b). An impressive *mahadvara* gateway with sixteen fine "lathe-turned" pillars and a superbly carved ceiling abuts the western wall, and a small gate leads down to the large tank on the eastern side (fig 76). Foekema compares the impression given by the wall with the one at Somnathapur and maintains that these two constitute the finest examples of Hoysala architectural surroundings[163]. The east-facing Chennakesava at Belur has a *prakara* wall. Some aspects were clearly added at a later date, including the magnificent *gopura* that was constructed under the Vijayanagar dynasty (fig 77). Hardy implies that some of the walls might also be later additions[164].

All the above examples have a paved courtyard, suggesting that this was common practice in walled complexes. Since the Lakshmidevi temple at Doddagadduvalli is the first documented Hoysala temple, and the Kesava at Somnathapur is one of the last, it is clear that the compound wall was a feature that spanned the Hoysala era. In the case of the Lakshmidevi it could be considered one of the first ways in which the Hoysalas asserted their individuality. The wall unquestionably enhanced the appearance of the temple complex adding splendour and unity and creating an illusion of increased size. However, once again other factors may have determined the building of a compound wall. Evidence from sculpture shows that music and dance played an important role in Hoysala society.

Collyer attributes the "Hoysala style" to Vishnuvardhana's interest in the arts[165]. His queen, Shantaladevi, was a dancer and singer and Collyer suggests that this influence is seen both in the sculptures and in the rhythmic movement of the star-shaped temple. Therefore it is conceivable that an important function of the *prakara* wall was to ensure privacy for the dancers and their audience of patrons and priests.

Fig 75a. Kesava temple complex, Somnathapur: Part of the cloistered prakara wall

Fig 75b. Somnathapur, Kesava: gateway (mahadvara or dvaramandapa) on the eastern side of the prakara wall, from outside the temple complex

115

Fig 75c. Somnathapur, Kesava: gateway (mahadvara or dvaramandapa) on the eastern side of the prakara wall, from inside the temple complex

Fig 76. Doddagadduvalli, Lakshmidevi: mahadvara gateway

Fig 77. Belur, Chennakesava: gopura

Safe from prying eyes: Hoysala mandapa

The importance of dance must also be taken into account when considering the temple *mandapas*. Hoysala temples tend to have a single *mandapa* with a closed rear part and open front part. Rarely do they have separate open and closed *mandapas*. Early Hoysala *mandapas* including the Chennakesava at Belur and the Hoysaleshwara at Halebid originally had open walls to the front. These halls are staggered squares, the staggering of the walls resulting in a "stepped-diamond" appearance. They have a parapet wall and seating bench to the open part. Half pillars rest on the bench to support the end of the roof, the rest being supported by full pillars. Later on the open walls were closed with solid stone blocks or perforated screens (*jalis* or *jalakas*) [166.] Settar attributes this to the Hoysala fondness for elaborate decoration on the outer walls but also to a desire to have subdued interior lighting[167]. This may be due to priestly and princely desire for privacy during ritual performances, including the "highly seductive dancing of the *devadasis*"[168]. Foekema regards Hoysala staggered-square, screened open

117

halls as the "architectural marvel of Later Chalukya and Hoysala architecture"[169].

The *vimana* of the Chennakesava is fronted by a very large staggered-square *mandapa* (fig 8a). There is only a small amount of solid wall at the rear of this temple. *Jalis* were added probably during the reign of Hoysala King Ballala II (1173-1220 CE). They are very intricately carved with geometric designs and puranic stories (fig 78). The doorways to the three temple entrances may also have been a later addition, perhaps to ensure extra privacy for performances on the fine dancing platform in the *mandapa*[170]. The two side-by-side shrines of the Hoysaleshwara at Halebid are linked by open *mandapas*, closed on the back wall only. Together they form the largest Hoysala temple. The total width of the combined open hall is forty-seven metres. It has an open front, later closed in with *jalis*, and closed back half.

Fig 78. Belur, Chennakesava: jalis

118

The Kesava temple in Somnathapur is unique in that it has a rectangular *mandapa* or *navaranga* instead of a square one, leading Foekema to suggest that symmetry is adversely affected (fig 79)[171]. Although it is usual for a *mandapa* to be based on a grid of nine *ankanas* and four pillars, the Kesava one is fifteen *ankanas* and eight pillars. Indeed the term *navaranga*, being based on the number nine, may be inappropriate. Radha Patel in fact only considers the back nine *ankanas* as the *navaranga*[172]. Foekema describes the open hall as having fifteen *ankanas*, which therefore includes the back closed part of the hall[173.] The three *garbhagrihas* lead off from the closed part of the *mandapa*, via an *antarala* (vestibule). The larger front part is open, though screened by several intricate, geometrically patterned *jalis*, divided by a narrow but deep *chadya*.

Fig 79. Somnathapur, Kesava: navaranga. Side view from the south.

The temples described above therefore illustrate the convention for Hoysala temples to have a single *mandapa* closed at the rear and screened at the front by *jalis*. In the case of the Hoysaleshwara and the Chennakesava temples the *jalis* were added later, but in subsequent Hoysala temples they were part of the original design. The term "open" *mandapa* hardly seems appropriate and indeed Hardy suggests they should be called semi-open *mandapas*[174]. However, not all Hoysala temples follow this plan. There are two notable Hoysala exceptions with completely open *mandapas*. These are the Viranarayana temple at Belvadi and the Ishwara temple at Arsikere. In addition some small temples, such as the pair at Marle, may only have a closed *mandapa* sometimes fronted by an open porch (fig 10c).

The plan of the Belvadi temple can be seen in fig 11a. The original Viranarayana shrine has a closed *mandapa* adjoining the *sukhanasi* in front of the *garbhagriha*, and then an open *mandapa*, which is a normal sized staggered square. A transverse open vestibule links the old and the new parts and the new open *mandapa*, like the old, is a staggered-square, forming a "stepped diamond." The two new *vimanas* are placed at opposite lateral points. Therefore the front point is the entrance and the back point links into the old part of the temple. The "new" open hall (*mukhamandapa*) is the largest in all of Hoysala architecture[175]. There are no *jalis* on this temple: the *mandapas* are truly open. The two lateral *vimanas* have *sukhanasis* that lead off immediately from the open *mandapa*, which makes them extremely unusual.

The Ishwara temple at Arsikere has a closed and an open *mandapa*. The closed *mandapa* (the *navaranga*), exceptionally, has rotated aedicules and a plan that Foekema refers to as a half star hall, unique in Hoysala architecture.[176] However, to appreciate the uniqueness of the closed hall, it must be considered as part of the overall temple plan (fig 12a). It shows not one, but two distinct structures – a closed hall and an open hall. The Ishwara open *mandapa* (*mukhamandapa*) (fig 80), like the *vimana*, is a sixteen-point star, instead of the normal staggered square, making it unique in Hoysala and probably in all Indian architecture. It has not been screened with *jalis*. Despite its perfect harmony with the rest of the complex, it also has something of an "add-on" quality, as it does not have to be passed through on the way to the *garbhagriha*. In this sense it is clearly not part of the symbolic journey from light into darkness, which is normally attributed to *mukhamandapas*. Its role seems to have become simply a gathering place for devotees, or a congregational hall. Hardy designates this *mandapa* as "spectacular"[177.] It does not have the usual ceiling squares or rectangles, and the hall cannot be counted in *ankanas*. The ceiling is supported by eight full-length pillars and by half pillars resting on the bench capping the parapet wall at each point of the star. The exterior *mukhamandapa* wall has no aedicular structure. However, Foekema suggests that a *hara* of *kutas* and rotated *kutas* was planned above the *kapota* leaving none of the domed roof visible[178].

Fig 80. Arsikere, Ishwara: mukhamandapa

121

The Hoysala preference for staggered-square *mandapas* filled in with *jalis* has been noted, apart from a few extraordinary exceptions. It has been suggested that the need for privacy during rituals or seductive dancing may account for the closing in of these *mandapas*. Was the *jali*, however, a distinct Hoysala feature? Perforated screens were a feature of Indian architecture dating back to the Lomas Rishi cave in the reign of Ashoka and the earliest surviving freestanding shrines from northern India during the latter part of the Gupta period (4th-6th century CE). In Karnataka the tradition goes back to the Early Chalukyas, the Durga temple being a notable early example (fig 81).

Fig 81 Pierced stone screen on the Durga temple in Aihole

The Later Chalukyas also had perforated screens. However, they used them around doorways rather than for closing in *mandapas*, which they preferred to keep open, using pillars and not walls to connect railings and eaves[179]. Fig 82 shows the *mukhamandapa* of the Yellammagudi (Yallama) temple at

Badami. It illustrates how an open *mandapa* developed from a simple porch, and it also shows perforated screens around the doorway. It does not, however, have the staggered-square configuration favoured by the Hoysalas.

Fig 82. Badami, Yellammagudi (Yallama): mukhamandapa

The Later Chalukyas also developed the use of the staggered-square for their open halls. However, Hardy lists few precedents before the late 11th century, an exception being the Siddeshwara in Haveri (fig 83), which may have been constructed in 1067-8 CE, although this date may refer to an earlier temple[180]. It appears that most coincided with the Hoysala era. Therefore the direction of influence is not clear-cut. Evidence suggests, however, that the Hoysala use of the perforated screen to "close in" open halls was not a Later Chalukya practice and was therefore distinct, or related back to some experiments of the Early Chalukyas.

Fig 83. Siddeshwara temple in Haveri

Giant wall-shrines: hot-line to the gods

Since much focus was on the outside of the temple, leaving the
dark interior to rituals and more private activities, it could be
argued that there was a call for the gods in the *garbhagriha* to
be externally accessible to devotees at all times. This may have
influenced the construction of the giant wall-shrines that are
present on a number of Hoysala temples. These are principal
wall-shrines cardinally placed on the *vimana* axes, much larger
than any other wall-shrines and attached to the *vimana* wall.
Hardy describes them as "almost fully emerged, as if having
burst out, almost free, virtually minor rather than miniature
vimanas usually containing two *garbhagrihas* one above the
other"[181].

Although Hardy considers the giant wall-shrine as a Hoysala
"special feature" it is not a universal feature. Moreover, it
cannot be said to be uniquely Hoysala. Sinha relates it back to
the North Indian concept of central *bhadra* offsets suggesting

124

the "swelling of the inner sanctum", which allows the divinity to manifest itself outside[182]. He suggests that this use of a North Indian concept within South Indian architectural vocabulary is a primary example of Vesara's originality.

The Later Chalukya Kasivisveshwara temple in Lakkundi (fig 84) is, according to Sinha, the first to use the northern concept of *bhadra* clusters with a deep niche. This allows "an image of the divinity to be housed within, as if in a real, freestanding shrine"[183]. It was subsequently taken up by other Later Chalukya temples in Karnataka.

Fig 84. Lakkundi, Kasivisveshwara temple, showing bhadra with niche

The *bhadra* of the Kalleshwara Temple in Kukkanur marked a conceptual shift, a reorientation within the Dravida language. The projecting *bhadras* expanded to the width of the inner sanctum, suggesting "an outward organic expansion of its space"[184]. They are aligned with the *garbhagriha* (plan: fig 85).

125

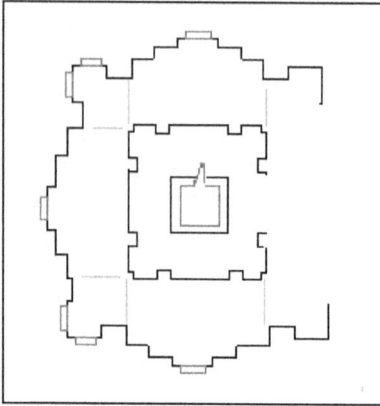

Fig 85. Kalleshwara Temple in Kukkanur: part of the garbhagriha showing alignment with offset badras

Of the twelve Hoysala temples in this study four have giant wall-shrines placed on one or more axes of the *vimana*. The earliest are those of the Chennakesava temple in Belur. Hardy concedes that this is a Nagara temple but maintains that they are nevertheless the starting point for the Dravida giant wall-shrines[185]. He describes them as *"mandapa vimana"* type halls being like an open *mandapa* but having a domed Dravida *kuta* superstructure. However, Foekema suggests that the domed superstructure is only an approximation of a Dravida *vimana*, apparently based only on the presence of *vedikas* and *kutas*[186]. The plan is square with a projection on each side and attached to the main *vimana* wall. They have two storeys, a *chadya* shading each storey. The underside of the *chadyas* shows imitation woodwork. Pilasters give the feeling of an open *mandapa*. They are remarkable for their size, and are additionally of interest because they display what Hardy describes as a prototype of the banded plinth[187]. Although it this is a tempting explanation, Foekema suggests that maybe they are not a prototype but "an echo", being inelegant and ill-fitting, thus indicating that they could be later replacements of earlier, smaller wall-shrines[188]. Fig 86 clearly illustrates this "stuck on" impression.

The Hoysaleshwara temple in Halebid also has orthogonal wall-shrines. Hardy suggests that they are conceptually close to those at Belur. Each has two niches, one above and one below its second *chadya*[189]. The Dravida nature of the shrine can be seen by the *vyalamala*, *kapota* and *kuta* roof elements of the superstructure, but there are also some small Nagara symbolic *vimanas*, as shown on fig 87. Just as in Belur, there is therefore a strange mixture of Dravida and Nagara elements. The central (western) *vimana* of the Lakshminarayana temple in Hosaholalu has three large wall-shrines at its central projections, which the other two *vimanas* do not have. They are all Dravida and have two niches. These can be seen on fig 14b. The Chennakesava temple at Marle has large central wall-shrines whose sides are not solid but filled in with *jalis* of a geometric floral design (figs 88 and 89). The wall-shrines also have a parapet in the form of a slanting seat back. Thus they imitate an open *mandapa*.

Fig 86. Belur, Chennakesava: Giant wall-shrine

127

Fig 87. Halebid, Hoysaleshwara Giant wall-shrine

Fig 88. Marle, Chennakesava: central wall-shrines jali screening the side

Fig 89. Marle, Chennakesava: Closed mandapa and vimana with wall-shrine

It appears therefore, that a northern concept within a Dravida setting, first exploited by the Later Chalukya dynasty, has become a defining feature on some Hoysala temples. Although large wall-shrines are sometimes seen on halls, it is those aligned with the cardinal axes of the *vimana*, and thereby associated with the *garbhagriha* by the symbolic manifestation of the deity through the *vimana* wall, that are regarded as a special feature of Hoysala architecture. However, they cannot be regarded as unique to the Hoysala era.

In short...

Certain elements of the temple layout were instrumental in defining the Hoysala style. The raised, stellate platform had never been seen before the Hoysalas introduced it, the *prakara* wall appears to have been an Early Chalukya feature that the Hoysalas reinstated. Although the staggered-square *mandapa* was not a new feature, the Hoysalas closed it with *jalis*, thus creating something original. The giant wall-shrines were a

Later Chalukya feature taken up by Hoysala architects. The temple layout may have been affected by the need to accentuate the size of the temple, and by the division between what took place inside and outside the temple. The outside was designed for public circumambulation, "reading" of the epics and communion with the gods within, necessitating access to exterior sculptures and shrines. The inside was geared towards the desire for privacy during priestly rituals and the activities and dances of the *devadasis*.

Chapter 6: So how original *were* the Hoysala temples?

That the Vesara temple did not originate with the Hoysalas, but in the northern Chalukyan realms of Karnataka is clear from the form and plans. Evidence refutes the suggestion that the Vesara temple was a hybrid of northern and southern styles, pointing instead to a localised form of the Dravida language. This would indicate that Hardy's term Karnata Dravida is appropriate. The complex stellate and staggered orthogonal plans of the Hoysala temples enabled them to develop in more ingenious ways. The stellate plan had rarely been seen before the Hoysala dynasty favoured it. It became very much a defining feature of the Hoysala style, enabling the added surfaces to be used for additional figure sculpture and maximising the effects of light and shade on the ornate carvings.

Decorative ornateness is a distinctive feature of Hoysala temples, although architectural ornateness was already found in Later Chalukya temples. An ornate temple is not necessarily architecturally more complex than a plain one. Although extensive figure sculpture is found on some Later Chalukya temples, it is nowhere as abundant as on some Hoysalas temples. Chalukya influence can be seen in early Hoysala figure sculpture. However, by the mid 12th century it had developed its own "squat", highly ornamented style. Study of this area is aided by the fact that Hoysala artists frequently signed their work, making it possible to trace their movements and their artistic development. Fundamental to the production of sculpture was the widespread use of chloritic schist, coupled with the localised skills of the Mysore sandalwood and ivory carvers.

Although granite temples were also built by the Hoysalas, chloritic schist or soapstone, first introduced by the Later Chalukyas, was found to be the predominant building material. All of the important Hoysala temples were built of soapstone, which sometimes involved transporting it over considerable distances. No documentary evidence was found to relate the height of the temple to the limitation of the soapstone's weight-bearing capacity; however, this could be a factor in the small size of the temples and the popularity of the raised platform.

Only one feature, the large, overhanging eaves or *chadya* separating the body of the temple from the superstructure, occurred in all temples. However, this also occurs on Later Chalukyas temples, and whilst being a distinctive feature of Hoysalas temples, it is not a unique feature.

Two features could be said to be unique to Hoysala architecture. These are the banded friezes and the second *chadya* occurring halfway down the body of the temple. Temples with banded friezes always have a second *chadya*, but temples with a second *chadya* do not necessarily have banded friezes.

To these "unique" features could be added the raised platform, which, while occurring once in a Later Chalukya temple and also being a feature of northern temples, took a completely different form in Hoysalas temples, following the contours of the temple's stellate plan. However, not all Hoysala temples stand on platforms. The platform is mainly, but not exclusively found in temples that have a banded frieze. As well as adding height, and delineating sacred space from the secular, the platform also facilitates viewing of the exterior sculptures, particularly the epic friezes. These are often under nine inches high in narrative form requiring circumamulation of the temple. Therefore the platform might be related to the importance of the temple.

The *prakara* wall is far more common in Hoysala than Later Chalukya temples, although it is not clear whether some walls have been removed from Later Chalukya temples. Evidence, however, points to a return to the tradition of the Early Chalukya dynasty, possibly encouraged by a desire for privacy as well as to enhance the size and splendour of the temple. Privacy may also be one of the reasons for closing-in with *jalis* open halls that owe their stepped-diamond layout to the Later Chalukya era. Hoysala temples only rarely have a closed hall as well as a separate open one, with several notable exceptions. The addition of *jalis* allowed private viewing of dance performances. Sculptural evidence and the presence of dance platforms in many temple *mandapas* indicate that dance was clearly an important feature of temple ritual. While such activities took place in the dark temple interior, opportunity for devotion was afforded on the exterior of the temple, not only by the sculptural abundance but also very often by the presence of giant wall-shrines at the cardinal points creating a direct link to the *garbhagriha*. These originated in the north and occur on some Later Chalukya temples. They were further exploited and developed by the Hoysalas but used selectively.

Dance is also reflected in the architecture of Hoysala temples, which create a spinning effect, not just in the stellate *vimanas* but also in the intricate "lathe-turned" pillars and reflective surfaces within the temple. "Lathe-turned" pillars are found in both Later Chalukya and Hoysala temples. Despite arguments to the contrary, it is probable that they were first turned on a lathe and finished by hand. These pillars are so complex, ornate, and universal in Hoysala temples that although not uniquely Hoysala they must be regarded as major contributors to Hoysala style.

Analysis of the twelve Hoysala temples found other features that would reward further study. Foremost among these is the interior of Hoysala temples, which has been largely neglected by scholars. However plain the exterior of a temple may be, Hoysala temples invariably have a richly carved and ornate interior. A feature of practically every Hoysala temple is the use made of the highly reflective surfaces of soapstone, which can be polished to a black shine of almost metallic quality. The Hoysala architects, as to some extent the Later Chalukya architects, made good use of this feature. The black pillars of the open *mandapa* at Belvadi have been polished to an incredible shine, and reflect off the shiny floor, accentuated by the huge size of the hall. "Lathe-turned" and stellate pillars in the Kesava temple at Somnathapur appear to spin, their polished surfaces enhancing the effect of movement through reflection and also creating an atmosphere inside the temple that could be seen as symbolic of the watery cosmos. The four magnificent central pillars in each *navaranga* of the Hoysaleshwara temple at Halebid reflect the light in their highly polished surfaces. The high shine on the floor of the circular dancing platform would have stimulated the senses during performances of dance by the *devadasis*.

While *panchalingeshwara* temples were not an innovation of the Hoysala dynasty, no prior instance in Karnataka of similar five-in-line plans has emerged, indicating that these may be a unique Hoysala feature. There is some debate regarding the number of *panchalingeshwara* temples constructed during the Hoysala era. Rangaraju lists only the ones at Somnathapur and

Govindanahalli. Foekema regards the Somnathapur temple as the only one. Settar has identified eight from late 13th century inscriptions. These could be in line with a resurgence of Shaivism at that time. At any rate, these unusual temples seem to have been situated at the heart of the Hoysala territories, and merit further investigation.

The question of syncretic temples also deserves further investigation. Unusually, the Lakshmidevi temple complex in Doddagadduvalli houses both Vaishnava and Shaiva *garbhagrihas*. Syncretic temples normally tended to be named after the Shaiva deity. It suggests that this period was one of some religious cooperation. It may also confirm that Lakshmi, when not depicted as the consort of Vishnu, transcends doctrinal considerations and is simply seen as the Goddess. However, its mixed iconography, and that of Arsikere and Govindanahalli lead some scholars to postulate a syncretic agenda to Hoysala temple development.

The relaxed attitude towards religion is further evidenced by the number of Jain temples built by the Hoysalas, including ones at Halebid and Shravanabelagola. Vishnuvardhana was a Vaishnava convert from Jainism. His queen, Shantaladevi, remained a Jain all her life. However, they freely associated their names with the Shaiva temple in Halebid, the largest and most opulent of all their temples, and constructed in their capital. The *Shivalinga* in the northern sanctuary is known as Shantaleshwara. The one inside the southern sanctum, which gives its name to the temple, is called Hoysaleshwara (referring to Vishnuvardhana as king of the Hoysalas). To the modern observer, it is something of a conundrum and illustrates the danger of making assumptions about the nature of sectarian interaction in mediaeval India. It is an area requiring further work.

A final point to be addressed is whether Hoysala temple architecture had any influence on the future architecture of Karnataka. Evidence suggests that the Vijayanagara successors to the Hoysala realms looked further south for inspiration, with the introduction of elements such as the *gopura* that they added to the Chennakesava temple in Belur. They did not build with soapstone and did not emulate the crowded, filigree sculpture of the Hoysalas, nor did they favour "lathe-turned" pillars. They did, however, continue the tradition of depicting epic narratives on the temple walls, though not in banded friezes. Had the Hoysala dynasty not been overthrown, the Hoysala temple may have continued to evolve. The last of these, the Kesava temple in Somnathapur has no wall-shrines at its cardinal points. Although not all Hoysala temples had them, in the case of the Somnathapur temple they seem replaced by a dynamic symmetry rather than simply left off, as if symbolically reabsorbed into the *vimanas.* Perhaps this was a further step in the search for perfect representation of cosmic forces.

At one end of the spectrum the line between Hoysala and Later Chalukya temples is blurred, which is hardly surprising considering the overlap both in time and place of the two dynasties. At the other end Hoysala temples with unique and unprecedented features such as a raised platform, frieze-bands, abundant sculptural galleries and a second *chadya* cannot be mistaken for anything else, and certainly amount to a distinct Hoysala style.

Postscript: The Hoysalas in the art history of the Indian temple

The pioneers

The temples of the Hoysala and other Karnataka dynasties were mentioned by 19th and early 20th century scholars in the first general works on Indian architecture. By the end of the 20th century these temples had become the focus of specialist studies. Some scholars have concentrated on transformation and evolution of architectural form in Karnataka, others have analysed Hoysala sculpture, others have looked at the social context and yet others have attempted to achieve a more holistic approach by concentrating on a few temples.

James Fergusson wrote his *History of Indian and Eastern Architecture* in 1876, the first significant general introduction to Indian architecture. Subsequent writers have built up on this early work submitting their own interpretations of the wide spectrum of Indian temples both architecturally and artistically. More recent writers have focused on specific themes such as a particular series of temples, or certain aspects of temple architecture or art.

Regarding the study of Hoysala temples, the early writers were important not least because they identified these temples as being worthy of inclusion in their works. Fergusson, certainly found Hoysala temples arresting, even if by declaring that the Chalukya style attained its fullest development and highest degree of perfection during the three centuries in which the Hoysala Ballalas held sway in the Mysore area, he was in effect denying Hoysala architecture a distinct classification. Fergusson's main interest lay in architecture. This is reflected in his praise for the play of light and shade facilitated by the horizontal and vertical lines of Hoysala temple architecture, an accomplishment he regarded as far surpassing that of Gothic architects[190]. Famously he compared the Hoysaleshwara temple in Halebid to the Parthenon, seeing them as polar extremes, the Parthenon pure intellect and Hoysaleshwara pure humanity but devoid of almost all intellect. He marvelled at Hoysala sculpture, calling it a "joyous exuberance of fancy" but seemed more impressed by the labour involved than the quality of the art[191].

Percy Brown's *Indian Architecture*, first published in 1942, is a general work on Buddhist and Hindu architecture. Like Fergusson he seemed uncertain about where to place the Hoysalas, calling his chapter "The Later Chalukya or Hoysala style (AD 1052- 1300)". However, he went on to say that it is not entirely satisfactory to suggest that all temples during this time were constructed under the Chalukya dynasty. He regarded the conformation of the Hoysala temple as distinct, despite maintaining that Hoysala temples were "not the work of a builder, but those of art craftsmen..."[192]. Brown regarded the Hoysala temple tower as "the keynote of the style" seeing plasticity in sculpture, but the architecture as without form or significant structure. While acknowledging their Dravida basis he maintained that the Mysore artisan transformed the style.

In her groundbreaking work of 1946, *The Hindu Temple*, Stella Kramrisch analysed in detail the religious symbolism underlying temple construction. Her metaphysical approach was based on the ancient Hindu texts. She did not analyse on a dynastic or chronological basis, therefore any specific reference to the Hoysala dynasty is limited. However, no subsequent studies of Indian temples can afford to ignore the conceptual basis presented in her work.

Later general works

Susan Huntington, in her 1985 book, *The Art of Ancient India,* makes a definite distinction between the Chalukyas of Kalyani and the Hoysalas. This book, as the name implies, is more concerned with art than architecture and therefore the architectural references are somewhat superficial, although from the content and descriptive aspect, it is a very inclusive work. In her view the Hoysalas had a mixture of northern and southern elements as well as being "highly distinctive". She sees the Hoysala tower as intermediate between that the pyramidal Dravida and the curvilinear northern type. She sees the towers' vertical tapered ribs as reminiscent of the northern forms, therefore she suggests a "hybridisation that some contend is the Vesara form of architecture"[193].

Huntington points out that the "ornate style" of Hoysala temples is in fact very much a minority: there are far more simple Hoysala temples than ornate ones. She comments that the Kesava temple at Somnathapur is "one of the finest Hoysala structures" on account of its "small size and gemlike carving"[194]. Other commentators have suggested that the carving is not of the quality of some other temples built by the Hoysalas, which illustrates that there is no such thing as objectivity in art. Interestingly Huntington describes the images in the three shrines at Somnathapur and mentions the Kesava image. This image is in fact missing, therefore possibly Huntington never actually saw the temple.

J C Harle's 1986 work, *The Art and Architecture of the Indian Subcontinent,* embraces both architecture and art of the whole subcontinent and this is achieved with some success. Harle sees Karnataka's contribution as distinctive, culminating in the

Hoysala style, which was a development from earlier styles. He refers to stylistic similarities between the Later Chalukya Someshwara temple at Gadag and the Hoysala temples, whose surviving superstructure he classifies as Vesara. He regards the Chalukya temples as the "only possible progenitor" to the Hoysala style but Hoysala temples were a development rather than a continuation, for Chalukya temples continued to be built at the same time as Hoysala ones (1986:261). He sees the Hoysala style as sub-regional and highly characterised. It developed in isolation hardly affecting the Later Chalukya style in the northern parts of Karnataka. Harle suggests that further research is needed to distinguish a pre-Hoysala or early Hoysala style.

Harle also saw Hoysala sculpture as of overriding importance in defining the "style". It reached its apogee at Belur, whose sculptures he parallels with those at Kajuraho. He maintains that the friezes around the bases of Hoysala temples correspond to northern and particularly western Indian practice, but were previously unknown in the south. However, the regional effect of ivory and sandalwood carving can be seen on Hoysala sculpture. Harle maintains it is characterised by "heavy jewellery and fat faces". He also suggests "frozen immobility" from which images "derive a certain grandeur"[195].

George Michell has made many specialised studies, including the Early Chalukyas and the Vijayanagara Empire. His 2000 work *Hindu Art and Architecture* incorporates the whole continent and covers two thousand years and as such its treatment of Hoysala temples is not interpretative and adds little to previous knowledge. He is included here because his work on the Early Chalukyas would be of great value to a wider study of the Hoysalas than is possible within the scope of this work.

The emergence of specialist studies on Hoysala temples

During the 1970s writing on Hoysala temples became more focused. Some dealt with the temples in general and others with particular aspects of them. Del Bonta's 1978 thesis, *The Hoysala Style: Architectural Development and Artists, 12th and 13th Centuries AD*, seeks to analyse the Hoysala style and evaluate its origins. His approach is both architectural and sculptural. Architecturally he divides the style into what he terms the Koravangala and Halebid types, the former being temples in the Later Chalukya tradition and the Halebid type exemplifying the ornateness and organisation widely associated with the Hoysalas. His sculptural analysis is mainly concerned with the latter. He analyses the work of particular sculptors, traced from inscriptions. His 12th century study concentrates on Halebid and Belur and his 13th century survey mainly involves temples were the sculptor Mallitamma worked. His analysis is therefore detailed but limited to a few temples, several of which are included in this study.

Adam Hardy's 1995 study, *Indian Temple Architecture: Form and Transformation*, focuses on architecture and its evolution. Hardy analyses the transformation of the Karnataka temple from the Early Chalukyas through to the end of the Hoysalas, approximately from 600 to 1300 CE. He argues that the direction of evolution is totally dictated by the Dravida architectural language. He dismisses the idea of a Nagara input in what he terms Karnata Dravida (in preference to Vesara) and refutes the suggestion that the temples could have evolved in any other way. Intrinsic to Hardy's analysis is the role of symbolism in temple design. He is particularly concerned with the centrifugal, vertical and horizontal forces unlocked by the staggering of aedicular structure and the stellate plans, all of which he sees as part of an attempt to recreate the disintegration and reunification of the universe, at the centre of which the deity presides in the *garbhagriha*.

He has concluded that the Hoysalas looked north to the Chalukyas in order to "establish their own school"[196] using in part artists imported from Northern Karnataka, as epigraphic evidence proves. However, these migrant artists employed local craftsmen, used to other materials such as wood, who transferred their crafts to working with soapstone. The style changes very little over the Hoysala period. Hardy states that it is difficult to date temples or put them into chronological order. He also notes the abundance of inscriptions and, unusually for India, the fact that sculptors signed their work and told something about themselves. Hardy does not seek to analyse the layout of the temple, and therefore does not have a great deal to say about aspects like the *mandapa*. He does not attempt any detailed analysis of sculpture, although he acknowledges that it impinges on architectural form, singling out the abundance of figure sculpture and the ornateness of Hoysala temples as two characteristics that distinguish them from Later Chalukya. Hardy maintains that Hoysala temples are more ornate than Later Chalukya temples but that the composition is no more complex.

He distinguishes between what he terms the mainstream and the non-mainstream strands of the mature phrase of Later Chalukyan temples. Mainstream is traceable back to the previous period. Non-mainstream draws from the same tradition but does not exhibit the same continuity of style. The boundaries between the two styles overlap and therefore the ascription to one or the other may be arbitrary. Geographically the mainstream were possibly patronised by the Later Chalukyan administration whereas the non-mainstream possibly by feudatories and their entourages, including the Hoysalas.

Hardy cites two characteristics that are indispensable but not unique to the Hoysala style. These are double eaves (i.e. the *chadya* in addition to the *kapota)*, and the diagonal *nasi* at the end of *shalas*. Four other features can be referred to as Hoysala specialities largely rooted in the Karnata Dravida of the Chalukyas:

1. The raised platform.
2. Giant wall-shrines.
3. The two-tier wall. The first *tala* is divided by a *chadya* canopy, slightly smaller than the one at the top of the wall.
4. The banded plinth: horizontal courses, which have friezes on them. They reinforce the horizontality of the two-tier wall and the raised platform.

Perhaps Hardy's most important contribution is the introduction into the language of Indian architecture of the concept of the aedicule, a miniature, roofed building[197]. The aedicule can be seen as the basic component of nearly all South Indian *vimanas* and has become an important tool for describing temple architecture.

Gerard Foekema made extensive studies of temple form in Karnataka in three works: *Hoysala Architecture* (1994), *A Complete Guide to Hoysala Temples* (1996), and *Architecture Decorated with Architecture* (2003), which concentrates largely on Later Chalukya temples. Unlike Hardy, Foekema has dealt with Later Chalukya and Hoysala temples discretely, rather than in one volume. However, he does not reject any connection between the two. Indeed Foekema connects Hoysala aedicules with the seventh century origins of Dravida architecture[198]. Hoysala architects, he maintains, continued in the Dravida mode but also made changes, and introduced Nagara aedicules. He classifies Later Chalukya and Hoysala temples as having strong stylistic unity, insisting it is correct to identify them as belonging one style. He does not see them as an intermediate group between northern and southern architecture, although geographically they can be seen as intermediate. They are predominantly Dravida with only the general outline being Nagara. He has found only five Hoysala temples with Nagara aedicules out of over a hundred.

Foekema uses Hardy's identification of the aedicule concept as an essential element in his descriptions. He classifies Hoysala aedicules in three ways: Old Dravida, New Dravida and Nagara. This classification is convenient, although the division is less to do with chronology than with appearance. All of them represent "a sudden alteration of the Dravida aedicule...during Hoysala rule"[199]. Star-shaped *vimanas* occur in all three types of Hoysala temple. New elements of Old Dravida aedicules are:
1. The *chadya* between the body and *kapota*
2. "Conspicuous figure sculpture decorating the body section"
3. The diagonal *nasi* to herald the presence of at least half *shala* aedicules.

Additional new elements of New Dravida aedicules are:
1. The second *chadya* on the body section
2. Six sculptured friezes of equal width replacing the lower mouldings.

Foekema argues against priestly involvement in temple development maintaining that architects and craftsmen alone created architectural articulation[200]. This had to be pleasing to patrons and priests, but not necessarily understand by them. He supports this argument by stating that no texts present a convincing alternative explanation

Both Hardy and Foekema entered into the debate on whether or not Karnataka temple forms show any Nagara influence. Ajay Sinha, in his 2000 thesis, published as *Imagining*

Architects, made studies of certain temples in Northern Karnataka, sometimes known as Vesara. Using Braudel's spatial scheme Sinha argues for "layered" maps- two maps interacting: local and regional. Microscopic regional changes affect local routines imperceptibly by a sort of network of wider influences. Sinha sees Vesara as a complex multilayered "region" based on its own networks of practice rather than an "intellectual periphery of north and south"[201]. He sees two strands of Vesara, one relevant to the northern temples and one to the southern (i.e. Hoysala) temples of Karnataka. The Hoysalas provided the connecting link in between north and south and artistic ideas flowed in both directions. Sinha singles out an emphasis on surface decoration as the main Hoysala characteristic. This is composed in clearly defined levels:

1. Base mouldings covered by layers of lacework and figural motives
2. Walls divided it into two sections with towers in the top section and prolific sculpture in the lower section.

Sinha sees differences between Western and Indian perceptions. He suggests that emphasis on architectural models and measurement (reduction, expansion, multiplication etc. of forms) in Vesara reinforces the temple as *Purusha*, the "universal principle at the foundation of all temples in India"[202]. However, he argues for a living relationship between Vesara architects and temples based on creative contributions to architectural traditions as well as on religious ideas. Therefore it can be seen that Sinha, like Hardy but unlike Foekema sees the search for religious expression in the evolution of architectural form.

Hardy, Foekema and Sinha concentrated largely on the architecture of Karnataka temples. However, other recent writers have made studies of the sculptural aspects.

Although S Settar, in his 1992 work, *The Hoysala Temples*, considers all aspects of Hoysala temples, it is clear that his emphasis is upon sculpture. Hoysala temples are some of the smallest to be found in India and Settar maintains that there are no others as rich in detail. He suggests two phases of sculpture: one coming to an end in Belur which he calls "the glorious days of sculptural art that began somewhere in the Later Chalukyan kingdom"[203]. The other phase began at Halebid and ended in Somnathapur: In the second phase the sculptures are more detailed, varied and abundant but not superior in style to those of the first phase. He suggests that the typical Hoysala characteristic of ornateness indicates a development in architecture but a decline in sculpture. However, the chief achievement of the Hoysala artist was that "he never fails to convey his message" regardless of whether or not he fails or succeeds artistically[204]. Settar talks about the *embarrass des richesses* but maintains that the elegance of movements, strength and vitality of the adolescent limbs and the grace and dignity of the face outshine this.

Settar acknowledges that architects saw themselves as Vishwakama, the heavenly architect, and that they built temples to imitate the abode of gods. He does not, however, attempt to link this to any developmental process, observing that Hoysala poets, like succeeding generations speculated endlessly on the "symbolic meaning and functional role" of some aspects of temple sculpture[205].

Some defining Hoysala elements mentioned by Settar include:

1. The *chadya* added between body and *kapota*.
2. The large wall image
3. Basement friezes
4. Chloritic schist
5. Pillars popularly known as "lathe-turned"
6. *Prakara* walls

7. The stellate appearance, which became the "chief hallmark" of Hoysala structures[206]
8. Sculpture governed by "uniform decorative, anatomical and stylistic principles"[207].

Kirsti Evans, in her 1997 work, *Epic Narratives in the Hoysala Temples*, has focused entirely on interpreting the epic narratives on thirteen Hoysala temples. Although there is a brief architectural description of each temple, the main emphasis is overwhelmingly on the sculptural detail. This work does not set out to integrate the two. Theories regarding the positioning and sequence of the carvings are generally not considered in the light of architectural considerations or social environment.

Rather than assuming that the way figures are depicted on the sculptures reflects the prevalent society Kelleson Collyer, in her 1990 work, *The Hoysala Artists*, cites abundant epigraphic evidence both in the form of signed sculpture and records left on stone steles. She is thus able to demonstrate, for example, that frequent reference to dance in temple sculptures and layout may be related to the interests of royalty and society at the time. Collyer's main interest lies in analysing the sculptures in terms of the artists who created them.

Dayananda Patel in his 1990 thesis, *The Kesava Temple at Somnathapur,* made a detailed analysis of sculpture of the Kesava and applied his findings to Hoysala society. He maintains that the Hoysala temples are applied art rather than true architecture. He has assumed that the artists modelled their sculpture on contemporary life rather than imagination or theological norms. He has not, however, provided much evidence for this. In her 2001 thesis, *The Life and Times of Hoysala Narasimha III*, M Radha Patel makes similar

147

assumptions based on several temples. However, she presents far more epigraphic evidence to give weight to her theories.

N S Rangaraju (1998) has approached his study of *Hoysala Temples in Mandya and Tumkur Districts* holistically. He has described each temple in detail, inside and out, architecturally and artistically. There are full descriptions of the temple layout and very detailed descriptions of the sculpture; however, descriptions of the form of the temple are brief. Whilst this is a useful reference work, it does not generally extrapolate new ideas from the results.

Glossary

For Volumes 1 and 2 combined

abhaya mudra: 'Fear not' gesture of reassurance and divine protection

acarya: DUALIST theologian

adhisthana: plinth or base of a DRAVIDA temple

Advaita Vedanta: Branch of the VEDANTA movement. MONIST theological movement regarding the self and the supreme universal entity as one

aedicule: miniature, roofed architectural element representing a building

Agamas: sacred doctrines not in the VEDAS; SHAIVA texts

Agrahara: braminical seat of learning

Ajivika: member of an ancient Indian sect of naked wandering ascetics

alpa vimana: basic VIMANA consisting of a single unit

Alvar: VAISHNAVA poet-saint

amalaka: fluted stone topping a temple tower, representing the amla fruit (Indian gooseberry)

Anantashayana: see SHESHASHAYANA

Ankana: square oil rectangular section of a *mandapa*

Antanta: see under SHESHASHAYANA

antarala: square antechamber in front of and linked to a temple's GARBHAGRIHA (sometimes also referred to as SUKHANASI, but actually inside the *sukhanasi*)

apsara: female protective figure, often associated with trees

arca: image of a deity

ardhamandapa: small, pillared porch

Arjuna: one of the five Pandava brothers: hero of the MAHABHARATA

ashtadikpalas: the eight directional deities, guardians of the heavens (Sanskrit: ashta=eight). Also called *DIKPALAS* or *LOKAPALAS*

astrabhadra: having eight BHADRAS or principal projections

asura: demon

asvamedha: horse sacrifice

Atharva Veda: the fourth and last of the VEDAS, largely composed of priestly spells and incantations

atman: the soul

avatar: incarnation (descent to Earth) of VISHNU (there are usually ten major ones). They appear when the earth is in deep trouble.

Avelokiteshvara: in Buddhism the compassionate BODHISATTVA

bhadra: central projecting offset

bhadra cluster: cluster of *bhadras* and flanking wall offsets

Bhagavata purana: ancient stories dealing with the life of KRISHNA

bhakta: a Hindu devotee and pilgrim

bhakti: devotion to and worship of a chosen god. A movement that started in South India in the 6th-7th centuries with the NAYANMARS and the ALVARS

Bharatanatyam: South Indian dance form

Bhima: one of the five Pandava brothers: hero of the MAHABHARATA

bindu: metaphysical term denoting an infinitesimal point where the divine and earthly meet

bodhisattva: A future Buddha who is awaiting enlightenment or has delayed Buddhahood in order to help others gain enlightenment

Brahma: one of the *trimurthi* (trinity of gods); the creator of the universe, who springs from the navel of VISHNU to begin the process of creation when Vishnu emerges from yogic sleep. (see SHESHASHAYANA or ANANTASHAYANA)

brahmadaya: grants given by kings in Karnataka

Brahman: eternal, unknowable Supreme spirit or universal entity from which everything originates and to which everything returns

Brahmasutra: Text relating to rules of worship, written in the form of aphorisms requiring commentary. Fundamental text of the VEDANTA movement.

brahmin: a member of the highest of the four main castes of Hinduism, the priestly caste (though these days not all male brahmins are priests)

caturkuta: temple with four shrines

cella: see *garbhagriha*

chadya : projecting eaves

chaitya: Buddhist assembly hall for group worship

chakra: discus of VISHNU

darshan: an audience with the divine; a meeting of the eyes of the deity and the devotee.

deva: god (*devi*: goddess)

devadana: land grant in Karnataka gifted directly to the deity

devadasi: women "married" to the temple deity who served as dancers, temple servants and prostitutes

dharma: socio-cosmic order; rules governing moral, legal and religious duty according to one's birth caste.

Dharmaraja: epithet given to Yudhisthira, eldest of the five PANDAVA brothers in the MAHABHARATA. Also used as an epithet for YAMA, god of death.

dhvajastambha: flagpole placed in line with the entrance to a temple.

diagonal nasi: term coined by Hardy (1995) to describe a NASI often found at the end of schematic SHALA roof elements

dikpalas: see ASHTADIKPALAS

Draupadi: the wife of the five Pandava brothers in the MAHABHARATA

Dravida: pertaining to South India (eg its people, customs and architectural styles). Here used to identify temple styles.

dualism: philosophy regarding the Supreme Entity (spiritual) and the Universe (matter) as two separate realities, with the Supreme Entity or God as omnipotent.

durbar: royal assembly

dvaramandapa: entrance gate

dvarapala: door guardian, ubiquitous on each side of shrine doorways and temple entrances.

dvikuta : temple with two GARBHAGRIHAS

ekakuta: temple with one GARBHAGRIHA

Entartete Kunst: degenerate art –German term used by the Nazis to describe art of which they disapproved

gada: mace or club: an attribute of VISHNU

gadyana: a mediaeval gold coin used in Karnataka and other parts of India

Gajalakshmi: The goddess LAKSHMI being lustrated by elephants. A water symbol often seen on temple entrance door lintels

gala: recessed element of a temple moulding

ganas: dwarves, of whom Ganesh is the leader

Ganesh: elephant-headed god, elder son of SHIVA and his consort PARVATI. Worshipped as 'he who overcomes obstacles' Homage is paid first to Ganesh before any undertaking

Ganga: The river Ganges. All rivers are personified as goddesses, with Ganga as the most important

garbha: The seed or germ of the temple

garbhagriha: inner sanctum, where the temple deity resides

gavaksha: horseshoe arch motif in NAGARA temples

ghanadvara: recess that resembles a doorway but is a solid-backed niche symbolically allowing the 'energy' of the deity to radiate through it.

gopi: a female 'cowherd' acolyte of Lord KRISHNA, whose 'personal' bond with the god is seen as the ideal relationship between deity and devotee.

gopura (gopuram): monumental South Indian temple gateway

hamsa: mythical goose, sometimes translated as swan

Hanuman: Monkey warrior, hero of the RAMAYANA

hara: row of linked band of linked roof elements (KUTAS, SHALAS, PANJARAS) in temple architecture

harantara: architectural linking section between HARA elements

hiranyagarbha: golden womb or golden egg – cradle of creation of the universe

istadevata: a worshipper's preferred deity chosen from a family of deities

jagati: NAGARA term for the whole platform on which a temple stands. Also lowest DRAVIDA plinth moulding

jali/jalaka: pierced stone window, patterned window grille

Jatayu: king of the vultures

Jatayusamhara: scene from the RAMAYANA in which the demon RAVANA fights and mortally wounds JATAYU, king of the vultures

Kadamba: type of temple named after a tribe in northern Karnataka

kalasha: finial or symbolic water pot on top of the temple tower. The last element to be installed, denoting completion of the temple

Kali: fierce goddess; form of SHIVA'S consort

Kalinga: name given to the temple type similar to temples occurring in Orissa

Kaliyuga: the age of the goddess KALI - the fourth and current YUGA ('world-age') in the cycle of creation. At the end of this final *yuga*, the universe will be destroyed to be created anew.

kalyana mandapa: marriage hall, where rituals celebrating the marriage of SHIVA and PARVATI are performed

Kamikagama: mediaeval theological texts from the ninth century onwards

kapota: overhanging cornice in temple architecture, eaves moulding

Karnata Dravida: term coined by Hardy (1995) to describe temples also known as Vesara

kirttimukha: the Face of Glory, a ubiquitous protective image found on temples across India

Krishna: avatar of VISHNU, widely worshipped across the world in his own right.

kudu: Tamil term for GAVAKSHA or NASI

kumba: pot, often features at the base temple door frames, symbolising water

kumbha : NAGARA plinth moulding

kuta: an ornamental 'dwelling' element in temple architecture, with a square, domed roof

kuta-stambha: pillar, usually embedded, crowned by a KUTA

Lakshmi: goddess of wealth, consort of VISHNU

linga (lingam): Undoubtedly of phallic origin now widely simply viewed as the symbol of SHIVA. Almost always the main shrine image in a SHIVA temple, usually in the form of a cylindrical shaft.

lingin: one who is identified in some way with the linga,

lokapalas: see ASHTADIKPALAS

madanakai: female bracket figure found in Later Chalukya and Hoysala temples

Mahabharata: monumental Sanskrit epic poem. Concerns the conflict between the five Pandava brothers and their cousins, the 100 Kaurava brothers for the conquest of upper India.. Contains the *Bhagavad Gita*, a dialogue between KRISHNA and ARJUNA including discourse on the role of duty, one of the most sacred texts in Hinduism.

Mahadvara: see DVARAMANDAPA

Mahishasuramardini: a form of DURGA created by the gods to destroy the buffalo demon Mahisha, when they were unable to do so themselves

makara: mythical water creature, VAHANA of GANGA among others

mandala: sacred plan upon which a temple building is based.

mandapa: pillared hall of a temple

mantra: sacred chanted verses believed to have symbolic power

matha: a religious institution of learning for boys attached to a temple

Mimansas: members of a movement rejecting image-worship in favour via sacrifice and other Vedic rituals

mithuna: loving couple, symbols of creation. In some, particularly Tantric temples, highly sexualised

moksha: release from the chain of rebirth and death.

Monism: philosophy regarding the Universe (matter) as merely a function of the Supreme Entity (BRAHMAN), and not a separate entity.

Mount Kailasha : mountain abode of the god SHIVA

Mount Meru: centre of the universe and home of the gods

mudra: hand gesture by which an Indian deity can often be identified

mukhalinga: LINGA with Shiva's face carved on it

mukhamandapa: open hall of a temple

mulaprasada: Nagara shrine

Mundaka Upanishad: philosophical poems written as MANTRAS used to teach meditation and spiritual knowledge regarding the true nature of Brahma and the Self (Atman).

murthi: form (of an image)

nadu: *a* group of villages

naga: snake, especially the cobra, sacred in Hinduism

nagakal: snake stone

155

Nagara: pertaining to North India (eg its people, customs and architectural styles). Generic name for north Indian architectural language. Here used to identify temple styles.

nakshatras: 28 constellations or lunar mansions that form the lunar cycle.

Nakula: one of the five Pandava brothers in the MAHABHARATA. Twin to SAHADEVA

Nandi: the white bull VAHANA of SHIVA. Also worshipped in his own right.

nasi: DRAVIDA term for GAVAKSHA, or CHAITYA horseshoe-shaped, gable-end arch form.

natya: dancing

navagraha: the nine planetary deities

navaranga: common term for a *mandapa* in Karnataka

Nayanmar: SHAIVA poet-saint

netronmilana: ritual of opening the eyes of a shrine image

New Dravida: term coined by Foekema to describe Dravida temples with certain innovations made by Hoysala architects.

nirguna: without quantities, formless

Orientalism: derogatory or patronising phrase coined in Colonial times to describe the study of Eastern civilisations.

padma: lotus, an attribute of VISHNU

padmagarbha mandala: temple plan known as the lotus womb

pancha: five (Sanskrit)

panchalingeshwara: term used to describe a temple with five LINGA shrines

pancharatha: term used by Foekema to mean a half star plan

panjara: Dravida miniature dwelling roof element - temple adornment, formed from the short side of a *shala*, decorated with a *nasi*

Phamsana: type of shrine with superstructure formed from a pyramid of KAPOTAS, sometimes identified with KALINGA or KADAMBA

PARVATI: consort of SHIVA

pitha: pedestal or small platform. Also plinth in north Indian architecture

pradakshina: clockwise circumambulation around the GARBHAGRIHA

pradakshinapatha: ambulatory path around the GARBHAGRIHA

prakara: wall surrounding a temple courtyard

prana: breath

prasad/prasada: food and flowers blessed by the temple deity

prasada: palace

pratistha: the infusion of divinity into an image, thus transforming it from material into divine substance

puja: act of worship

Puranas: texts containing the mythological stories of the gods including the creation myths.

Purusha: original man, cosmic force; cosmic man whose dismembered body was the source of all creation

Ramayana: monumental Sanskrit Indian epic narrating the banishment of RAMA and SITA, Sita's abduction to Sri Lanka and the wars fought by Rama with HANUMAN to retrieve her

Rama: Avatar of Vishnu. Hero of the RAMAYANA. King of Ayodya.

Ramayana: Great Sanskrit epic poem. Concerns the story of the god-king Rama's rescue of his wife SITA from the clutches of RAVANA, the demon-king of Lanka.

ratha: chariot used in temple festivals to carry the UTSAVA MURTHI around the town and the temple

rathapatha: processional way where large RATHA are stored

Ravana: demon in the RAMAYANA

saguna: a formless deity that has taken 'form' as a shrine image

Sahadeva: One of the five Pandava brothers in the MAHABHARATA. Twin to NAKULA

saka: Indian date system: Saka Era (78 CE = year 0)

samanta: Hindu prince of a minor territory; princedom

Samhitas: collections of sacred doctrines ; VAISHNAVA texts

sandhara: (shrine) with a PRADAKSHINAPATHA, or ambulatory path around the GARBHAGRIHA

Shaiva: pertaining to SHIVA

Shakti: 'divine energy' personified as the goddess, particularly Parvati, the consort of SHIVA

shala: barrel-vaulted architectural element

shalabhanjika: divine maiden of Buddhist origin, usually clinging to a tree

shanka: conch shell: one of VISHNU'S attributes

Shesha: see under SHESHASHAYANA

Sheshasayana: (Also ANANTASHAYANA) representation of VISHNU reclining on the 'endless' serpent SHESHA (also known as ANANTA), floating on the cosmic ocean, recommencing the cycle of creation at the end of his yogic sleep.

shikhara: domed finial of a South Indian VIMANA, also whole superstructure of a North Indian MULAPRASADA

Shiva Nataraja: Lord of the Dance, one of the best-known 'aspects' of SHIVA, particularly in South India. Shiva's auspicious dance of creation and destruction took place in Chidambaram in Tamil Nadu.

Shiva: one of the TRIMURTHI (trinity of gods); widely worshipped, seen as the deity who will destroy the world at the end of the KALIYUGA in order for it to be regenerated anew

Shivalinga: see LINGA

Shrivaishnavaism: a VAISHNAVA theological movement, emphasising the role of the goddess Shri. Inextricably linked with the ALVARS and perfected by the Brahmin philosopher Ramanuja in the 11th/12th centuries.

Sita: consort of RAMA

snapana: temple ritual of bathing the god

sodasatra: sixteen-point star plan

stambha: pillar

sthalavrska: sacred tree

sthanu: everlasting or pillar-like

sthapati: architect

stupi: crowning element of a temple tower. Also STUPIKA

stupika: crowning element of a temple tower. Also STUPI

sukanasi: exterior of the ANTARALA; literally 'parrot's bill, extending from the VIMANA

Surya: the sun god, chief of the planetary deities

svayambhu: 'self-manifested' Refers to a shrine-image created by nature, but also to the transcendent, 'not created' BRAHMAN

syncretic temple: temple with shrines to both SHAIVA and VAISHNAVA deities.

tala: storey or tier of the VIMANA

tirtha: a place of pilgrimage, the fording of the river, a mental crossing to a state of inner realisation

torana: elaborate, arched motif framing many images; also arched gateway

tribhanga: triple-flexed stance used in figure sculpture

trikuta: temple with three GARBHAGRIHAS

Trimurthi: trinity of three major deities: BRAHMA, VISHNU, SHIVA

triratha: staggered square plan with three projections on each side

trishula: trident – attribute of SHIVA and those in the SHAIVA pantheon

unjal seva: the ritual of rocking the deity in a swing

utsava murthi: transportable deities, usually made of bronze, wood or clay

vahana: 'mount' of a deity; also a reflection of character of the deity.

Vaikhanasagama: South Indian sub-texts of the AGAMAS

Vaishnava: pertaining to VISHNU

varnas: the four original castes: BRAHMINS (priestly caste), Kshatriyas (warriors, rulers , nobility), Vaishyas (merchant and farming caste), Shudras (labourers)

vastumandala:symbolic temple plan recreating the structure of the universe

Vastupurusha: (see also PURUSHA) enormous man created by Brahma who grew so big he overshadowed the Earth and was then pinned down by VISHNU and SHIVA and the ASHTADIKPALAS in a symbolic act of sacrificial dismemberment.

Vastupurushamandala:. MANDALA based on the pinned-down body of the VASTUPURUSHA

Vastushastras: Hindu architectural texts based on oral traditions *such as the* VASTUVIDYA

Vastuvidya: Vedic oral traditions and texts pertaining to architecture

Vedanta: a movement in Hindu philosophy centred on ideas from philosophical texts, the *Upanishads*

Vedas: Sacred hymns and prayers from around 1000 BCE, originally orally transmitted

vedi / vedika: architectural element of temple moulding on a DRAVIDA temple, representing a railing

Vesara: term for some temples in Karnataka that are thought by some scholars to be neither pure NAGARA nor pure DRAVIDA, though this is disputed by others

Vibhishana: a hero of the RAMAYANA. Brother of RAVANA. Joined forces with RAMA and later became king of Lanka

vicitracitta: 'multifarious', implying divinity

vimana: term used for the whole shrine, including SHIKHARA, in South Indian temples

Vishnu: one of the TRIMURTHI (trinity of gods); widely worshipped, seen as the deity who maintains the status quo and creates order in the world. When this order is threatened by evil 'he descends to earth as an AVATAR to restore stability.

Vishnucaturvimsati: 24 cosmic forms of Vishnu

Visistadvaita: a school of Hindu philosophy that sees the BRAHMAN as one but also accepts the multiplicity of souls within the world (qualified non-dualism)

viyala: See YALI

vyalamala: an architectural moulding element consisting of bands of mythical animal representations

yajamana: temple's patron, symbolic sacrificer

yaksha/yakshi: semi-divine nature beings

yali: leonine creature forming the base of a pillar, particularly in Pallava and Chola temples and their successors

Yama: god of death

Yuga: world-age

Bibliography for Volumes 1 and 2

ALI, D. In MICHELL G (ED) (1999) *Eternal Kaveri,* Vol 51 No.1, September 1999, Mumbai, Marg Publications

ANNASWAMY, T.V. (2003) *Bengaluru to Bangalore,* 1st edition, Bangalore, Vengadam Publications

ARAMUGA N. (1851) The Proper Way to Worship at Siva's Temple. In:LOPEZ, D. S. *Religions of India in Practice,* Princeton, New Jersey, Princeton University Press.

BANERJEA, J. (1956) *The Development of Hindu Iconography,* 2nd edition, Calcutta, University of Calcutta.

BAXANDALL, M. (1988) *Painting and Experience in Fifteenth Century Italy,* Oxford, Oxford University Press

BLURTON, T. R. (1992) *Hindu Art,* 2001 edition, London, The British Museum Press

BRANFOOT, C (2005) *Regional Past, Imperial Present: Vijayanagara Temple Architecture In Karnataka.* Paper presented at: *The European association of South Asian Archaeologists Biennial Conference* July 2005, London

BRANFOOT, C.. (1999) Tiruchirappelli and the Sacred Island of Srirangam: in Michell G (ed) *Eternal Kaveri,* 1st edition, Mumbai, Marg Publications

162

BROWN, P (1942) *Indian Architecture (Buddhist and Hindu)*, Bombay, D B Taraporevala Sons & Co. Pty. Ltd

CHAKRABARTI, V. (1998) *Indian Architectural Theory*, 1st edition, Richmond, Curzon Press

COLLYER, K (1990) *The Hoysala Artists: Their Identity and Styles,* Mysore, Directorate of Archaeology and Museums.

DALLAPICCOLA, A. (2002) *Dictionary of Lore and Legend*, 1st edition, London, Thames & Hudson

DAVIS, R. (1997) *Lives of Indian Images*, 1st Edition, Princeton NJ, Princeton University Press

DAYANANDA PATEL, T (1990) *The Kesava Temple at Somanathapura,* Delhi, Agam Kala Prakashan

DEL BONTA, R J (1978) *The Hoysala Style : Architectural Development and Artists, 12th and 13th Centuries AD,* Unpublished thesis (PhD), University of Michigan
Delhi, CBS Publishers & Distributors
Delhi, Indira Gandhi National Centre for the Arts

DESAI, V. & MASON D. (eds.) (1993) *Gods, Guardians and Lovers: Temple Sculptures from North India 700-1200,* Ahmedabad, Mapin Publishing

ECK, D. (1998) *Darsan: Seeing the Divine Image in India,* 3rd edition, New York, Columbia University Press

EVANS, K (1997) *Epic Narratives in the Hoysala Temples,* Leiden, Brill

FERGUSSON, J & TAYLOR, M (1866) *Architecture in Dharwar and Mysore*, London, John Murray,

FERGUSSON, J (1876) *History of Indian and Eastern Architecture.*1997 edition of 1910 revision, Delhi, Low Price Publications

FISHER, R.E. (2002) *Buddhist Art and Architecture,* London, Thames & Hudson

FOEKEMA, G (1994) *Hoysala architecture : medieval temples of southern Karnataka built during Hoysala Rule,* New Delhi, Books & Books

FOEKEMA, G (1996) *A Complete Guide to Hoysala Temples*, New Delhi, Abhinav Publications

FOEKEMA, G (2003) *Architecture decorated with Architecture: Later Medieval Temples of Karnataka 1000-1300 AD,* New Delhi, Munshiram Manoharlal Pvt Ltd

FRITZ, J.M. & MICHELL, G. (2003) *Hampi,* Mumbai, India Book House Pvt.

FULLER, C.J. (1992) *The Camphor Flame: Popular Hinduism and Indian Society,* 1st edition, Chichester, West Sussex, Princeton University Press

GROVER, S. (1980) *Buddhist and Hindu Architecture in India,* 2nd edition 2003, New Delhi and Bangalore, CBS Publishers

GURURAJACHAR, S. (1974) *Some Aspects of Economic and Social Life in Karnataka 1000-1300 AD,* Mysore, Prasaranga, University of Mysore

164

HARDY, A. (1995) *Hindu Temple Architecture: Form and Transformation,* New Delhi, Indira Gandhi National Centre for the Arts

HARLE J.C. (1986) *The Art and Architecture of the Indian Subcontinent: Pelican History of Art*, 2nd Edition 1994, New Haven and London, Yale University Press

HEITZMAN J. (1995) *State Formation in South India 850-1280.* In KULKE H. (Ed.) *The State in India 1000-1700* pp162-195, Delhi, Oxford University Press

HUDSON, D.D. (1995) *How to Worship at Siva's Temple.* In LOPEZ, D. S. *Religions of India in Practice,* Princeton, New Jersey, Princeton University Press.

HUNTINGTON, S. (1985) *The Art of Ancient India,* New York and Tokyo, Weatherhill.

KEAY, J. (2000) *India, A History Volume 1,* 2003 edition, London, The Folio Society

KESHAVA NAIK, H.P. (1998) *Some aspects of Feudal Elements in the Vijayanagara Polity 1336-1565 AD,* Mysore, Prasaranga, University of Mysore

KRAMRISCH, S. (1946) *The Hindu Temple Volumes 1& 2*, 1991 edition, New Delhi, Motilal Banarsidass Pvt. Ltd.

KRAMRISCH, S. (1954) *The Art of India,* 1965 edition, London, Phaidon Press Ltd.

KRISHNAPPA .M.V. (1994) *Social and Economic Conditions of Karnataka 400 –1000 AD,* 1st edition, Director, Mysore, Prasaranga, University of Mysore

KULKE, H. & ROTHERMUND, D. (1986) A *History of India*, 2nd edition, London, Routledge

KULKE, H. ed. (1995) *The State in India 1000-1700*, Delhi, Oxford University Press

LOPEZ, D. S. ed. (1995) *Religions of India in Practice*, Princeton, New Jersey, Princeton University Press

MAHESHWARI, S. & GARG, R. (2001) *Ancient Indian Architecture*, New Delhi, CBS Publishers & Distributors

MASON, D. in DESAI, V. & MASON D. (eds.) (1993) *Gods, Guardians and Lovers: Temple Sculptures from North India 700-1200*, Ahmedabad, Mapin Publishing

MAXWELL, T.S. (1997) *The Gods of Asia: Image, Text and Meaning*, 1st edition, Delhi, Oxford University Press

MEISTER, M.W. *Fragments of a Divine Cosmology.* In DESAI, V. & MASON D. (eds.) (1993) *Gods, Guardians and Lovers: Temple Sculptures from North India 700-1200*, Ahmedabad, Mapin Publishing

MICHELL, G (Ed) (1999) *Eternal Kaveri*, Vol 51 No.1, September 1999, Mumbai, Marg Publications

MICHELL, G. (2000) *Hindu Art and Architecture*, 1st edition, London, Thames & Hudson World of Art

MICHELL, G. (1977 rev.1988) *The Hindu Temple*, University of Chicago

MICHELL, G. (2002) *Pattadakal*, New Delhi, Oxford University Press

RABE, M.D. In LOPEZ, D. S. (ED) (1995) *Religions of India in Practice*, Princeton, New Jersey, Princeton University Press.

RADHA PATEL, M (2001) *Life and Times of Hoysala Narasimha III*, Mysore, Prasaranga university of Mysore

RANGARAJU, N. S. (1998) *Hoysala Temples in Mandya and Tumkur Districts*, Mysore, Prasaranga university of Mysore

RANGASWAMIAH, G R (1972) *Organisation of Trade and Commerce in the Hoysala Period*. In SHEIK ALI, B: *The Hoysala Dynasty*, Mysore, Prasaranga, pp 161-168

ROWLAND, B. (1953) *The Art and Architecture of India: Pelican History of Art*, 1967 edition, Harmondsworth, Penguin Books Ltd.

SETTAR, S (1992) *The Hoysala temples*, Bangalore, Kala Yatra

SHESHADRI, M (1972) *Hoysala temple Architecture*. In SHEIK ALI B: *The Hoysala Dynasty*, Mysore, Prasaranga, pp 181-190

SINHA, A J (2000) *Imagining Architects: Creativity In The Religious Monuments Of India*, Newark, University of Delaware Press

STEIN H (1995) *The Segmentary State: Interim Reflections*. In KULKE, H. ed. (1995) *The State in India 1000-1700*, Delhi, Oxford University Press

STEIN, B (1998) *A History of India*, Oxford, Blackwell

STEIN, B. (1978). *All the King's Mana. IN Perspectives on Kingship in Mediaeval South India*. In RICHARDS J. F. ed.

Kingship and Authority in South India, Madison, University of Wisconsin Press

STIERLIN, H. (2002) *Hindu India,* Cologne, Taschen GmbH

TADGELL, C. (1990) *The History of Architecture in India,* 1st edition, London, Architecture Design and Technology Press New York, Columbia University Press

TARTAKOV, G & DEHEJIA, V. (1984*) Sharing, Intrusion and Influence:,* In Artibus Asiae 45/4, Zurich, Museum Rietberg

TILLOTSON, G.H.R. (1998) Foreword. In CHAKRABARTI, V. *Indian Architectural Theory,* 1st edition, Richmond, Curzon Press

ZIMMER, H. (1946) *Myths and Symbols in Indian Art and Civilisation,* 1972 edition, Princeton, Princeton University Press

Index of Temples in this volume

Index of photographs and illustrations

Govindanahalli, Panchalingeshwara temple. Small wall images Fig 42. p72

Govindanahalli, Panchalingeshwara temple: *dvarapala* Fig 43. p73

Groundplan: half-star plan. Fig 19b. p37

Groundplan: simple square plan. Fig 19c. p37

Groundplan: sixteen-point full star plan formed by rotating a square. Fig 19a. p37

Halebid, Hoysaleshwara Giant wall-shrine Fig 87. p128

Halebid, Hoysaleshwara temple plan Fig 9b. p17

Halebid, Hoysaleshwara temple showing the two *vimanas* Fig 9a. p17

Halebid, Hoysaleshwara temple: Dancing Ganesh. Fig 52. P81

Halebid, Hoysaleshwara temple: Mahishasuramardini. Fig 51. P81

Halebid, Hoysaleshwara, Halebid door lintel Fig 32. p61

Halebid, Hoysaleshwara: "rafters" and beading on *chadya* Fig 68. p100

Halebid, Hoysaleshwara: *dvarapala* Fig 41. p72

Halebid, Hoysaleshwara: frieze band Fig 57 p86

Halebid, Hoysaleshwara: Joist ends related to *vyalamala* visible beneath the *makara* frieze. Fig 24b. p45

Halebid, Hoysaleshwara: *kapota* shape discernible behind epic frieze Fig 24c. p46

Halebid, Hoysaleshwara: showing *chadyas* and a wall shrine. Fig 67. p100

Halebid, Hoysaleshwara: steps to platform flanked by miniature shrines. Fig 74. p110

Halebid, Jain temple showing "Lathe-turned" pillars in Hoysala temples Fig 69d. p103

Halebid, Kedareshwara temple, frieze panel Ravana mortally wounds the vulture-king, Jatayu, (Ramayana) p93 Fig 62e

Halebid, Kedareshwara. frieze panel: The death of Bishma, (Mahabharata): Fig 62d, p92

Haveri, Siddeshwara temple Fig 83. p124

Karnata Dravida temples distribution, showing material used for construction. Fig 30. P59

Khajuraho, Devi Jagadamba temple, Fig 72. p110

Kikkeri, Brahmeswara: showing "Lathe-turned" pillars in Hoysala temples Fig 69a. p104

Kukkanur, Kalleshwara Temple: part of the *garbhagriha* showing alignment with offset badras Fig 85. p129

Kundgol, *mandapa* of the Later Chalukya Sambhulinga temple Fig 70.p107

Lakkundi, Kasivisveshwara temple, showing *bhadra* with niche Fig 84. p128

Lakshneshwar, Someshwara temple: porch Fig 63a. p96

Lakshneshwar, Someshwara: porch rafters Fig 63b. p97

Major 12th and 13th peninsular Indian dynasties Fig 4. p6

Marle, Chennakesava and Siddeshwara temples Figs 10b and 10c. p19

Marle, Chennakesava: central wall-shrines *jali* screening the side Fig 88. p132

Marle, Chennakesava: Closed *mandapa* and *vimana* with wall-shrine Fig 89. p132

Marle, plan of the Siddeshwara temple Fig 10a. p18

Marle, Siddeshwara, showing "Lathe-turned" pillars in Hoysala temples Fig 69b. p104

Pattadakal, Virupaksha: porch showing the *chadya*-like eaves Fig 64. p97

Road between Javagal and Arsikere Fig 15c. p29

Schematic roof elements. Left to right: *kuta, shala, panjara.* Fig 23. p44

Somnathapur, Kesava temple complex,: Part of the cloistered *prakara* wall Fig 75a. p117

Somnathapur, the Kesava temple Fig 18a. p35

Somnathapur, Friezes at the Kesava Temple, Fig 61. p92

Somnathapur, Hoysala Stele outside the Panchalingeshwara temple Fig 17c..p33

Somnathapur, Kesava temple: Janardhana icon p84, Fig 53

All photographs and illustrations by the author unless otherwise stated

Endnotes

---

[1] Radha Patel 2001:21
[2] Rangaraju 1998:16
[3] Huntington 1985:555
[4] Collyer 1999:64
[5] The Hindu 25th November 2004
[6] Radha Patel 2001:21
[7] Collyer 1990:12
[8] Collyer 1999:65
[9] Sinha 2000:32
[10] Stein 1998:131
[11] Kulke & Rothermund 1986:130
[12] Dayananda Patel 1990:15
[13] Collyer 1990:33
[14] Ibid p78
[15] Hardy 1995:244
[16] Del Bonta 1978:70
[17] Ibid 1978:71
[18] Hardy 1995:250
[19] Del Bonta 1978:77
[20] Collyer 1990:90
[21] Harle 1986:262
[22] Del Bonta 1978:80
[23] Evans 1997:195
[24] Srivatsa (*personal communication*, 6th August 2005)
[25] Hardy 1995:338
[26] Settar 1992:212 and 214
[27] Foekema, 1994:188-9 and *personal communication* 30th
     September 2005.
[28] Foekema 1994:107
[29] Hardy 1995:324
[30] Rangaswamiah 1972:161-165

[31] Sheshadri 1972:184
[32] Rangaraju 1998:113
[33] Collyer 1990:148
[34] Foekema 1994:129
[35] Hardy, 1995:332
[36] Ibid p333
[37] Foekema 1994:168
[38] Radha Patel 2001:134
[39] Rangaraju 1998:133
[40] Foekema 1994:118
[41] Rangaraju 1998:131
[42] Settar 1992:201
[43] Ibid p53
[44] Based on Settar, 1992:216
[45] Foekema, 1994:32
[46] Del Bonta 1978:75
[47] Ibid p73
[48] Hardy, 1995:250
[49] Foekema 1994:129
[50] Foekema, 1994:32
[51] Settar 1992:149-50
[52] Rangaraju 1998:114
[53] Hardy 1995:250
[54] Foekema 1994:39
[55] .Dhaky 1977
[56] Sinha 2000:21-22
[57] Ibid p29
[58] Hardy 1995:8
[59] Foekema 1994:243
[60] Kramrisch 1946:292
[61] Foekema 1994:244
[62] Based on Foekema 1994: 20
[63] Foekema ibid
[64] Foekema 1994:87
[65] Hardy 1995:252
[66] Ibid pp288 - 289
[67] Foekema 1994
[68] Del Bonta 1978:70

[69] Collyer 1990:43

[70] Kramrisch 1946:290

[71] Sinha 2000:23

[72] Hardy 1995:8

[73] Dhaky, in Sinha 2000:118

[74] Sinha 2000:119

[75] Hardy 1995:323

[76] Rangaraju, *personal communication,* 22nd September 2005

[77] Harle 1986:263

[78] Settar 1992:134

[79] Rangaraju, *personal communication,* 22nd September 2005

[80] Foekema 2003:49

[81] Settar, 1992:147

[82] Rangaraju 1998:24

[83] Hardy 1995:15

[84] Ibid p159

[85] Ibid p258

[86] Ibid p260

[87] Ibid p357

[88] Ibid p245

[89] Foekema 1994:165

[90] Hardy 1995:245

[91] Foekema 2003:35-37

[92] Del Bonta 1978:76

[93] Ibid p70

[94] Settar 1992:250-251

[95] Because the Chennakesava is a living temple, the Kesava image inside the shrine that the dvarapalas are guarding, is so enveloped in cloth and garlands that it is almost totally obscured.

[96] Settar 1992:253

[97] Foekema, 1994:100

[98] Del Bonta 1978:127

[99] Settar 1992:259

[100] Ibid p277

[101] Foekema, 1994:129

[102] Del Bonta 1978:8

[103] Ibid p165

[104] Settar 1992:287

[105] Ibid p201
[106] Del Bonta 1978:179
[107] Collyer 1990:23
[108] Rangaraju (1998:121) has suggested that
[109] (Foekema, 1994:158)
[110] (Sheshadri, 1972:189)
[111] Collyer (1990:91-92)
[112] Foekema 1994:167
[113] Evans 1997:7
[114] Collyer 1990:158
[115] Settar 1992:266
[116] ibid 261
[117] Settar 1992:285
[118] Evans 1997:197
[119] Harle 1986:267
[120] Settar 1992:259
[121] Collyer 1990:126
[122] Foekema 2003:70
[123] Ibid, 1994:22
[124] Evans, 1997:243
[125] Hardy 1995:248
[126] Harle 1986:262
[127] Foekema 1994:132
[128] Hardy 1995:254
[129] Settar 1992:221
[130] Evans 1997:210
[131] Foekema, 1994:167
[132] Ibid p168
[133] Hardy, 1995:356
[134] Ibid p:98
[135] Ibid p:332
[136] Foekema, 1994
[137] Ibid, 1994:21
[138] Ibid, 1994
[139] Ibid p230
[140] Dayananda Patel, 1990:20
[141] In Fergusson & Taylor, 1866:47-8)
[142] Brown, 1942:140

[143] Settar, 1992:134

[144] Collyer, 1990

[145] Langeveld, 2005: *personal communication*

[146] Hardy, 1995:262

[147] Ibid p246

[148] Meister, 1993:103

[149] Hardy, 1995:346 and Foekema, 2003:49

[150] The term *vedi* is inappropriate here, since Nagara temples do not have *vedikas* (Foekema, 1994:24 and *personal communication*, 2005)

[151] Hardy, 1995:254

[152] ibid

[153] Rangaraju, 1998

[154] Foekema, 1994:118

[155] Hardy, 1995:325

[156] Settar (1992:219-220)

[157] Rangaraju, 1998:131

[158] Hardy 1995

[159] Ibid p339

[160] Settar, 1992:130

[161] Rangaraju, *personal communication:* 2005

[162] Hardy, 1995:245

[163] Foekema, 1994:122

[164] Hardy, 1995:476

[165] Collyer, 1990:41

[166] The *jalis* have been included in this chapter, rather than in the chapter on sculpture, since they are such an intrinsic part of the Hoysala *mandapa*.

[167] Settar, 1992:152

[168] Grover, 1980:208

[169] Foekema, 1994:49

[170] Del Bonta, 1978:126

[171] Foekema, 1994:223

[172] Radha Patel, 2001:128

[173] Foekema, 1994:222

[174] Hardy, 1995:246

[175] Foekema, 1994:111

[176] Foekema, 1994:87

[177] Hardy, 1995:246

[178] Foekema (1994:87 and *personal communication,* 2005)

[179] Settar, 1992:152

[180] Hardy, 1995:330

[181] Ibid p248

[182] Sinha, 2000:111

[183] Ibid p109

[184] Ibid p168

[185] Hardy, 1995:256

[186] Foekema, 1994:100

[187] Hardy, 1995:253

[188] Foekema, 1994:100

[189] Hardy, 1995:253

[190] Fergusson, 1910:448

[191] Ibid p449

[192] Brown, 1942:139-140

[193] Huntington, 1985:566).

[194] Ibid p 571

[195] Harle, 1986:267

[196] Hardy, 1995:243

[197] Ibid p18

[198] Foekema, 1994:12

[199] Ibid p18

[200] Ibid, 2003:10

[201] Sinha, 2000:24

[202] Ibid p30

[203] Settar, 1992:165

[204] Ibid p318

[205] Ibid p179

[206] Ibid p131

[207] Ibid p249

GOLDENFORD

www.goldenford.co.uk

www.ingramcontent.com/pod-product-compliance
Lightning Source LLC
Chambersburg PA
CBHW031955040426
42448CB00006B/374